HYPNOSIS IN PSYCHOTHERAPY

Understand yourself and resolve your emotional problems

N B Morley

Act 3 Publishing

Copyright
1985
©
Act 3 Publishing
67 Upper Berkeley Street London W1

ISBN 0 948068 00 0

Designed by Clive Sutherland

Printed and bound in Great Britain by
Redwood Burn Limited, Trowbridge, Wiltshire

NICHOLAS BOLAND MORLEY is a trained, qualified, registered, experienced psychotherapist, hypnotherapist and counsellor. A graduate of The Psychotherapy Centre and a Member of the British Hypnotherapy Association, he's been in practice for many years.

Familiar with group therapy as well as one-to-one therapy, he uses only the latter because he finds it more effective.

He's one of the few practitioners designated to take on as patients people who wish to take the training course at The Psychotherapy Centre, which involves first of all having extensive therapy oneself. He also takes on other patients.

Born in South America, he speaks Spanish as well as English. He has participated in BBC broadcasts in both these languages. He has also given numerous talks on hypnotherapy and given lectures on the training course at The Psychotherapy Centre.

His writings have been published in The Psychologist, the Psychotherapy Review and You.

CONTENTS

	Preface	7
1	Basic instincts / evolution of man / survival	9
2	Pre-birth / birth / birth and therapy	18
3	Feeding / defecating	30
4	Sex / incest taboo / homosexuality / impotence / orgasmic inability / sex with animals / improved sex life from an outside stimulus	39
5	Aggression / paranoia / jealousy	67
6	Parental attitudes	82
7	Choosing a sex partner and getting married / why do people have children?	86
8	The conscious and the unconscious / dreams	91
9	Symptoms, causes and treatment	97
10	Starting therapy; enquiries / the consultation	112
11	The therapeutic situation / the trial period / patients benefitting from a single session	121
12	Young patients and their parents and relatives / couples seeking therapy	129
13	Patients expressing their feelings to their parents	139
14	Results and follow-ups	145
15	Two cases of hypno-analysis	154
	Further reading	188
	Index	189

PREFACE

Psychotherapy is a term which covers the many forms of psychological treatment for emotional problems. This includes the use of hypnosis, in which case the treatment can be referred to as hypnotherapy. In this book, except for the last chapter, for the sake of simplicity and convenience I have restricted myself to using the word psychotherapy unless I'm specifically referring to hypnotherapy or hypno-analysis. I don't always use hypnosis.

Many books on the subject of psychotherapy tend to be of an esoteric nature, usually written by therapists. Unless the reader has some knowledge of psychotherapy, they make difficult reading. In addition they are usually riddled with analytical theory and jargon, which I have tried to avoid.

My purpose in writing this book is to make an involved subject understandable to people with little or no knowledge of psychotherapy. What I say in parts of the book may be obvious to some readers, but the whole book should be readable by all. I have confined myself to the basic principles of the psychotherapy I use, basing most of the material on my own experience as a therapist, giving examples where possible.

Although I see both male and female patients, I have, for convenience, used the male pronoun when I refer to a patient unless it's a specific female patient I'm referring to. I have also used the male pronoun when referring to babies or children, unless they are specifically female. The same applies when I refer to therapists, who can be of either sex.

Where I refer to parents, I include surrogate parents.

This book isn't a complete step-by-step guide to psychotherapy and hypnosis, but an introduction to these subjects.

The views expressed by me in it are my own and are not necessarily all shared by my associates.

I have used plain, unambiguous language, the language I use in talking with my patients, and in quoting my patients I have not censored or toned down what they said. If a psychotherapist were inhibited, euphemistic, devious or obscure in the way he expressed himself, this would discourage his patients from being frank and honest, which they must be if they are to get the best results in their therapy.

ONE

Basic instincts

Many years ago, at a period when I had ambitions to become a farmer, I was studying on a farm in Sussex. One day I had to go out into a field to find a cow which had not returned with the rest of her herd. After some searching I eventually found it in some dense bushes. It had just calved, the wet calf and after-birth lying on the ground. The cow was licking the calf and, as I watched, began to eat its own after-birth. Having consumed it, the cow then licked the grass clean of any vestiges of the birth. This behaviour struck me as odd until I realised that this was an instinct left over from the time when cattle were undomesticated. A newly born animal is an easy meal for a hungry predator, which explains why after giving birth is a time when most female animals become aggressive. The after-birth could have attracted predators. The protection instinct in many farm animals has not disappeared in spite of thousands of years of domesticity.

Other domestic animals also preserve their natural instincts. Dogs have a strong territorial instinct which makes them good guardians of property. In my native South America my father had a ranch where there were three canine territorial boundaries. The house dogs had one section, the gardener's dog had another and the workers' dogs had theirs. They all lived peacefully, providing the dogs kept to their boundaries. The only time these dogs ganged up was when a stray dog happened to appear on the ranch, when all the dogs would set on the unfortunate animal, tearing it to pieces.

Taking a dog for a walk may necessitate many stops when the dog urinates. This is a method for some animals in the wild to mark their territory. Although the domestic dog has no need to mark his territory, the instinct is still there.

In these examples of the cow and the dog the basic instinct, in a domestic situation, serves no purpose, but both animals behave as if it does. Instincts die hard, especially when they involve survival.

Man as a species is governed by instinct although we have reached a stage in our development when we forget that we are animals with basic drives. Our three basic instincts are self-preservation, reproduction and the herd instinct. It is important to bear this in mind when discussing behaviour, as instincts have such a major influence on our behaviour, even though this may not always be apparent to us. Looking back to the past, to the evolution of man, helps us to understand some of our present behaviour.

Life expectancy in humans is something under a hundred years. In evolutionary terms a hundred years is so short a time that it is not considered; it is too short to measure. Our normal perception of time tends to be measured in units of up to a hundred and occasionally a thousand years. Christ lived about two thousand years ago, calendar years being numbered from that time. Two thousand years is a long time. Before that, sense of time becomes difficult to visualise. The Chinese dynasties began in about 2,800 BC while the Egyptian dynasties started about 3,200 BC, our earliest recorded history. If we go back further, much further, we eventually come to a thousand thousand years, ie a million years. This is the unit of time used when dealing with evolution. First signs of life on earth began to appear about 3000 million years ago, according to Richard E Leakey and Roger Lewin. The most distant of Man's identifiable ancestors (the first hominid) appeared about ten million years ago. This ancestral line led to modern humans, beginning with Homo erectus, which emerged some two million years ago. For man to have survived this long, instincts have been essential and are so ingrained that they are difficult, if not impossible, to remove.

Even so, man has not been around very long compared to the time there has been life on earth. If we assume, as an analogy, that life on earth has been in existence for one year, man has been around for only a few hours. This helps to give some proportion to time in regard to the evolution of man.

Evolution of man
Man is a relative newcomer to life on earth but, during the evolution of man, many changes have taken place. Two changes are believed to be of paramount importance.

The first change was when our ancestors renounced their arboreal way of life and climbed down to the ground. We still are not certain why they broke away from the other primates and came down from the trees. They were adapted to live above the ground, that way of life being much safer than living on the ground. There is no evidence that there was a lack of food in the trees, which would have been a good reason to come down to earth. From the information available there seems no obvious motive why man chose a terrestrial form of life. We can only guess. One possible explanation is adventure, an innate compulsion to explore, a basic need for stimulation. Or it could have been caused by savannas replacing some of the forests, necessitating some species to live on the ground. But this is only speculation; perhaps we shall never know.

Once down from the trees, our ancestors stood up on their hind legs and their bodies adapted to a terrestrial existence. By standing on their hind legs, they freed their hands for other things such as the manufacture and manipulation of tools. Also, their diet changed. Meat was included and as a species they became omnivorous. This was a significant change. Our ancestors learnt to hunt, becoming aggressive predators. Life on the ground was more dangerous, but with this change of diet a much greater freedom was obtained, as they were independent of any single source of food. By eating meat, less time was spent on feeding, as protein conversion from vegetation necessitates large intakes of food. More time was then available to dare and to explore. One must remember that these changes would have taken place over millions of years.

The second important change in the evolution of man took place much later, only about half a million years ago. Our brain got bigger, much bigger, and it remains a mystery why it grew so large. It is much bigger than we need, and most of it remains unused. Lyall Watson in his book 'Supernature' says: 'We have acquired this incredible organ at the expense of several others, and yet we use only a minute part of it. What was the hurry? Why have we raced along this line of development so fast? We could certainly have got by with much less. At the moment, we are like a small family of squatters who have taken over a vast palace but find no need to move beyond the comfortable, serviced apartment in one corner of the basement'.

This increase in size was mainly due to a second brain emerging – the thinking brain. The thinking brain imposed itself on the smaller instinct brain, which became controlled and taught to function according to the wishes of the thinking brain. This eventually led to behaviour which was acceptable to the larger brain. Man is a social animal and to live together in harmony we must establish order in one way or another. We couldn't survive without it. Anarchy doesn't work.

This enormous increase in our thinking capacity brought with it many problems. This imposition, one brain on the other, leads to conflict: our natural impulses against ordered behaviour. Balance between these two forces can be attained, where we are free to do as we wish, but within the bounds of whichever society or religion we happen to belong to. Not only does this behaviour differ between societies, but it also changes within the same society. Our Victorian forefathers would be shocked at our comparatively liberal views today, particularly regarding sexual behaviour. Yet in many ways we are still largely a repressed society.

The achievement of this balance between instinct and ordered behaviour occurs mainly in childhood when the child is at home. Unfortunately, the pupil can only be as good or as bad as the teacher, and many parents make bad teachers. An unbalanced parent will inevitably produce an unbalanced child.

If you go to the zoo and watch monkeys, you may come to the conclusion that they are preoccupied with sex. If you study monkeys in the wild, in their natural habitat, you will notice that it is territorial dominance they are primarily concerned with, not sex. In the zoo the conditions are not natural. Monkeys have no territory to defend; the cage is theirs, and after the hierarchy has been established, there is no more contention. In the wild the story is different. Many species are preoccupied with self-preservation, in particular ensuring the protection of their territory, mainly from challenges by others of the same species. For many species, territory is vital for survival.

We live in a human zoo, and sex is very important. Unfortunately, for one reason or another, and I shall say more about this later in the book, many people are sexually repressed. In our everyday lives, most of us have few problems with territorial rights; we don't often have to fight to retain our house or our land. The law gives some protection. We have developed a society which enables us to live together in harmony. Social rules are made for the benefit of us all. Behaviour in any given society can be likened to a game of rugby, where we are free to do as we please providing it is within the rules of the game.

At the same time, within all of us lurks the sexual, aggressive animal, and if we attempt to hold it down it will erupt in one form or another. Sometimes these eruptions are shown in symptoms, either mental or physical. We have to learn to express our feelings in positive terms, or problems will arise. We are aggressive, sexual animals, whether we like it or not, and some of us don't like it. Some of us prefer to ignore it and pretend it isn't so.

Emotional problems have probably always existed but as the complexities of life have increased, with greater social and moral demands upon us, and increasing remoteness from basic instincts, many people have problems created in their childhood relationships with their parents. These problems usually plague them for the rest of their lives. As a species we may survive, but are we getting healthier in our emotional lives?

Survival

No species would survive without reproducing. A species can reproduce either sexually or asexually. Reproduction by binary fission doesn't depend on sex. The amoeba reproduces simply by dividing itself in half. Thus the amoeba never dies – unless it gets eaten or is destroyed. What it gains by longevity it loses by not being able to enjoy sex.

The advantage of asexual reproduction is that survival can be maintained by rapid reproduction in a suitable element. A bacterium can split in two every twenty minutes and a single female aphid can produce, without sex, hundreds of thousands of offspring in one summer. In asexual reproduction, the offspring are all genetically identical. However, once conditions become harsher, the advantages of sexual reproduction become apparent. Having variable offspring enables natural selection of the species to come fully into effect, some offspring being able to survive and ensure the continuity of the species. Being able to reproduce asexually as well as sexually, like the aphid, gives the advantage of reproducing at high speed when conditions are favourable, but reproducing variable offspring when conditions are harsh.

Man reproduces sexually. The offspring takes genes

from both parents, some genes being dominant and some recessive. If you have blue eyes for instance, and you mate with someone with brown eyes, the offspring are likely to have brown eyes. Blue-eye genes are recessive.

Animals that cannot or do not adapt will, by necessity, die out. Changes in inherited characteristics are called mutations. These are chance results from breeding which Charles Darwin called natural selection. It's these changes which give us the vast differences in living creatures and enables certain species to survive better than others. We are told that zebras have stripes because at one point in their evolution, by genetic chance, stripes appeared in some of the animals and, because of the camouflage value, they survived. They were able to adapt to their environment. Other species like the dinosaur, unable to adapt, did not survive.

Man has probably survived because of his intelligence. The human being is no match for many animals on a purely physical basis. He is not the fastest runner, nor is he the strongest or most ferocious. He swims very slowly and he cannot fly. But he does have the advantage of being the best all-rounder. Natural selection in animals enables the fittest to survive; the sick perish while the healthy survive. This is a quick and easy solution to a disease, or to a genetic malformation. Natural selection also encourages a species to develop means of survival. The slowest antelope will die, the fastest will live. This system has worked well in the wild. But modern man has less natural selection. This is not healthy, although the lack of natural selection is balanced by our healthier living. Modern hygiene has helped to eliminate most of the traditional killers like cholera, pneumonia, typhoid and pleurisy. We are physically healthier than at any time in our evolution. A high standard of living and improved environmental conditions ensure a healthier life. A modern baby has virtually a 100% chance of survival. In the wild, the chance of survival of a young animal is low. In the 'developed' parts of the world, fit or not, we survive – and the species survives – unless we cannot reproduce. The emotionally sick also survive with the emotionally fit. The only exception is if a person is too emotionally disturbed to be able to pair up with someone of the opposite sex and reproduce. We don't eliminate emotional problems by natural selection any more than we eliminate physical problems.

Because our thinking brain is so complex, and because it has to exist with our basic instincts, it takes a long time for a human being to mature emotionally. Physically, we are well behind other species. We cannot reproduce until we are 12 or 13 years old. This is almost a lifetime for some animals of our size. Yet physically we are well ahead of our emotional development, which does not reach maturity until the late teens.

TWO

Pre-birth

We may see the mind as divided into two parts: the conscious and the unconscious. The conscious mind is the part we are aware of.

We may also view the mind as consisting of the higher mind, or intellect, which is mostly conscious, and the lower mind, which is partly unconscious. The lower mind is the part where we have our innate feelings and desires. This is the animal in us. Our breathing, heart-beat, digestion and other natural functions are controlled by this area of the mind. Over some of our natural functions, most of us don't have any direct control. You can't directly alter your digestive pattern or heart-beat, except through hypnosis, unless you are one of those yogis who, after many years of meditation, are able to exert some influence on these functions. In his book 'Alternative Medicine', Robert Eagle says: 'In 1971 Dr Elmer Green performed a number of tests on an Indian called Swami Rama. As well as demonstrating telepathic and psychokinetic skills (he was able, amongst other things, to make a cyst appear on his thigh, disappear and reappear on other spots), Swami Rama, while connected to an ECG, showed that he could alter his heart-beat at will from 66 beats a minute, up to 94 and back to 52'.

Emotional problems occur when the higher and lower parts of the mind come into conflict, usually from the higher mind trying to control our innate desires. Our higher mind has shot ahead at such a fantastic speed that it has completely overtaken and sometimes obscured our basic instincts. We became predatory aggressors five or six million years ago, or longer, while our brain started getting larger about half a million years ago. It's difficult to believe that we can obliterate millions of years of inbred behaviour in a few thousand years. Although our thinking brain is in charge of most of our actions, the lower mind is the stronger force, even if we are not always aware of its influence. The intellect often tries to overrule the lower mind, but without success: repressed feelings will appear in one form or another.

Some people believe that man is not aggressive by nature. Adlerians are convinced of it. This is a rationalisation. Some anthropologists are divided on this issue. Raymond Dart, Konrad Lorenz and Robert Ardrey have been proponents of the idea that man is innately aggressive, while Richard Leakey and Roger Lewin argue that this is dangerous fiction. I believe the latter group are confusing normal healthy aggression with hostile aggression associated with emotional disturbance. I will deal with this later in the book. If you can't accept your aggressive feelings, it's an escape to believe that you have none or that you must not let them out. Our thinking brain is relatively young and our animal brain is relatively old.

With good healthy childhood upbringing, we develop a balance between our higher and lower minds. This balance is essential for us to function as adequate human beings. We speak of well-balanced people if all is well, and unbalanced people if there is something wrong. Learning this balance takes time and is normally achieved in the development of child to adult. The human, when he's born is, more than any other animal, completely dependent on his mother, physically as well as emotionally. The father also plays a role, but at the beginning the mother is all important.

It is only in recent years, starting with the discoveries spearheaded by Freud and others, that we have learned the importance of the parent–child relationship. Parents are of paramount importance to children. The effect of bad parents or no parents can be disastrous, as I will show later in this book. Our behaviour in life is largely governed by our relationship, as children, with our parents. A sobering thought. We react to people in much the same way as we reacted to our parents, as well as copying some of our parents' traits. Our learning starts at birth and continues especially during our formative years. In discussing behaviour, we have to start at the beginning, with the baby.

At conception, certain characteristics are passed on from the parents to the child: our genetic inheritance. It is not certain how much of the parents' mental characteristics are passed on, but intelligence, for instance, is largely inherited. One of the problems of research into human behaviour is that we can't experiment on human beings in ways which might harm them; we can only rely on what evidence is available to us, and often this is not very much. Some observations have been made with identical twins who have happened to be brought up in different circumstances, comparing them later in life.

After conception, the foetus is no longer influenced by genetics. It lives in a 'warm bath' for nine months, with little else to do but grow. It's fed by the mother through the placenta, where blood from the mother transmits nutrients to the blood of the baby. There are no nervous tissues connecting mother and child, so that there is no direct communication in this way with the baby. Some mental disorders can be wholly or partly inherited, but not emotional problems. It's often assumed that emotional problems are inherited. This may suit some people's thinking: 'I'm made like this, I can't change.' It gives them an excuse to do nothing about their problem. One reason for the belief that emotional problems can be inherited is that quite often children display the same symptoms as their parents. I have not come across any evidence that children can inherit neurotic symptoms from the parents. A child may have an emotional problem which manifests itself in a stutter, for instance, and often one finds that one of the parents also stutters. The fact that children often *imitate* their parents to the extent of displaying the same neurotic symptom is important for the therapist to bear in mind when treating patients. Patients will often take on the traits of the practitioner, whom the patient will see as a parent figure.

One young female patient told me:

'I've suffered from hay fever all my life. So has my father.'

Another middle-aged female patient, who stopped getting hay-fever, reported:

'I started getting hay-fever when I was six years old. My father and brother also get hay-fever.'

Birth

Many women fear giving birth. Traditionally, giving birth is a painful affair. Most women expect to feel pain, as when going to visit the dentist. Much of the fear of a painful birth can be caused by what mothers tell their daughters. Any pain that is experienced in childbirth is made worse by the tension caused by fear. One patient, in her forties, who had been married three times, told me:

'I didn't want children, partly because of what my mother told me. She had a bad birth with me. I ripped up all her insides. This made me frightened.'

Giving birth should be a natural function. Grantly Dick-Read made his name with his book 'Childbirth Without Fear'. He believed that there was no need for pain in childbirth, which may sound extreme to some people. Nevertheless, women do experience pain in childbirth, although how much is natural pain, and how much is caused by psychological factors, is open to question.

One of my female patients had given birth to three boys. She had her first child when she was 31, a birth that did cause her some trouble. Two years later she had her second. 'I had Paul in ten minutes,' she told me. 'I could have got up and danced!'

Childbirth is usually easier after the first child. This may be a combination of a more relaxed attitude by the mother and a repeated physical function which the body may find easier to perform.

Using 'painkillers' during childbirth can be dangerous. Some 13% of mothers who die in childbirth do so because of medical drugs or gases used for anaesthesia. Not only can drugs affect the baby as well as the mother, but anaesthetising a woman in labour is difficult, one of the most difficult tasks an anaesthetist has to perform. In fact any drugs administered to a pregnant woman, either before or during labour, can be dangerous, if not lethal. The 7,000 surviving thalidomide victims in the world, mostly in West Germany, are a grim reminder of how a drug taken by a pregnant woman can affect the foetus.

Various factors affect the ease or otherwise of a birth. Age is relevant, as is physical condition. The younger and fitter the mother is, the easier the birth should be. Bone structure is also important: a wide pelvis helps. But perhaps attitude of mind is most important: the more relaxed you are the better. Being well-informed about childbirth is also essential. Antenatal classes can be of great value. Being well-prepared and knowing what will happen takes away much of the anticipated fear.

After nine months in the womb, the baby experiences the first traumatic experience of his life: the birth. From a safe warm container, he is suddenly ejected, with great thrusts, into a strange, cold environment. It's not surprising that sometimes one of the first actions of a baby is to cry. The baby's lifeline, the umbilical cord, is cut. The unconscious mind is already functioning when the baby is born. He starts breathing, and the by-pass holes in the heart close, enabling him to oxygenate his own blood supply. He also feeds, sleeps and defecates. He would not survive without these natural impulses. Many animals in the wild are standing up within minutes of birth. They have to, in order to survive. A human baby may not walk until he's almost two years old. By this age some animals our size are reproducing. Human babies are helpless.

Birth and therapy
Birth and pre-birth experiences have been fashionable in certain types of therapy in recent years. Some

therapists as well as some patients firmly believe that emotional disorders are caused by birth. I have not encountered any evidence that a birth can cause emotional difficulties, which leads me to believe that there is no substance in this theory. R D Rosen agrees. In his book 'Psychobabble', he says: 'To assume that abreacting the birth trauma solves life's problems is an insult to one's intelligence and a displacement of complex responsibilities onto a comforting single cause.'

Other people are intrigued by the possibility of having lived in a previous life. At the Psychotherapy Centre we receive many enquiries from people wanting to regress to birth and beyond, hoping to discover that they have been on earth in a previous life. A 23-year-old woman of Indian parentage consulted me for emotional problems. She said that she was nervous and shy in company. She told me she was sure she had been on earth in a previous life and was certain that because of something that had happened then she was in her present condition. She believed she was being punished for something she'd done. She had guilt feelings, probably caused by repressed wishes. Attributing this to a previous life could be one way of dissociating herself from her problems. These patients are difficult to help as they have an unrealistic approach to therapy.

There have been published accounts of people who have remembered what they have thought to be an event in a previous life. Some believed they had even been in other countries and spoken in different tongues. These beliefs remain unproven. What appear to be extrasensory experiences often turn out to have a more mundane explanation. Some people experience déjà-vu. They feel that they have seen something or been somewhere before, when this wasn't logically possible. This can help the belief that they have been there or seen something in a previous life. Déjà-vu has been explained by the fact that sometimes the brain receives two messages from the same stimulus, one message just before the other. By the time the second message arrives the first has already registered and thus gives the impression of a previous experience.

One explanation that I heard which could explain apparent 'experiences in a previous life' was made by an American. He suggested that as babies (and he did give some evidence for this) some people may have heard a story or a radio programme or a television broadcast which was instilled in their minds. These recollections were stored in the unconscious and remained there as inconsequential information. This information may remain there and never become conscious and consequently the person concerned will never be aware of it. But in certain conditions this stored material may become conscious. If the information deals with some past history, it could be interpreted as experience in a previous life. This does seem a plausible explanation. It may or may not be correct or there may be other explanations. The fact remains that the human mind is a very complex machine and not yet fully understood.

I have not come across any evidence, among my patients, of birth or pre-birth memories, although some of my patients have remembered incidents that occurred a few weeks after birth. I don't regress a patient back to a specific time of his life but, with the patient in hypnosis, I suggest he will remember the causes of his problem. This may or may not relate to early childhood. If a patient believed that a particular type of recollection was expected of him he could unconsciously invent an appropriate one.

I have found that many patients like to believe that their problems relate to a particular experience and if this is uncovered their problems will disappear. Unfortunately, this is seldom the case. I did have one patient, a woman, who had a cat phobia and recovered after four sessions as she was able to recall the reason of her phobia, an experience when she was a baby in a pram. I shall give a fuller account of this case later. Problems are usually caused over a number of years and take time to sort out.

Many memories from childhood are traumatic. Often, because they are traumatic, they are repressed and this can cause problems later in life. Part of therapy is to release these pent-up feelings.

If a patient does appear to remember an unpleasant childbirth it could be claimed that the memory is authentic. But is it? I have found that many patients fantasise a lot, even in hypnosis. People often want to remember things as they think they were, or would like them to have been.

I have found that many of my patients, nearly all of them women, have dreams of being pregnant or of giving birth. I have come across only one male patient who dreamt of being pregnant. These birth dreams have always related to the treatment the patient was undergoing. The baby is usually the patient, or rather the baby in the patient which has never been allowed to come out or express himself. The patient is giving birth to his repressed childish feelings. Many parents do not allow their children free expression of their feelings. I have heard parents tell their child 'Don't be childish!'

This is often the parent projecting his or her own childish feelings onto the child. If the parent feels it's not acceptable to express his or her own feelings, the child won't be allowed to express *his*.

A dream with a good birth is usually a sign that treatment is progressing well while a bad birth or an abortion is a bad sign. Something is wrong. A bad birth can be an indication that the patient is going to break off treatment. In this respect dreams can often tell the therapist what the likely prognosis of therapy will be, which may enable him to take the necessary steps to rectify any problem that may be arising. Quite often, by encouraging the patient to express any negative feelings, a crisis is averted. If the therapist doesn't recognise a particular problem (often caused by the therapist not having sorted his own problems out), the patient may discontinue treatment.

Here are some examples of positive dreams:

A 47-year-old widow who was frigid and didn't like men told me these dreams:

'I was having a baby.'

'I had a healthy baby. I was protecting it.'

'There was a baby girl in a pram. I'm looking after it. I don't know where it lives. A social worker tells me: "You haven't been looking after it well".'

Another widow, a 58-year-old nurse with no children, told me:

'I saw a baby running away. I tried to catch it.'

'There was someone having a baby. The head was all bruised.'

'There were some baby rabbits. They were all huddled up. They were getting cold. They were dying. I caught them in time. I'm glad.'

A 39-year-old divorcee who was frigid and had one

child:

'I had a baby. The father didn't know.'

I find that some patients have dreams in which complications arise at or after birth. This is usually an indication that they are doubtful about treatment. Here are some examples:

A 27-year-old married woman said that she did not want any children. She was frigid and wasn't interested in sex. She told me this dream:

'I was in hospital, in a private ward. I was going to have a baby. I didn't want it. I was telling everyone to get out. I said I would do it myself.'

A 20-year-old girl, who was getting married in four years' time, had only had sex once and it wasn't very good. She came to see me because she was afraid of people being ill or vomiting.

'I was in hospital having a baby. All the doctors and nurses were friends. I asked for the baby. They couldn't find it. There was a muddle.'

A 34-year-old married woman who was not keen on sex and was undecided about having children:

'I gave birth to a baby. The process was completely painless. It surprised me. I kept losing it. I was carrying it around. It was like a cat. It kept hiding. People told me it would grow. I was frightened I might tread on it.'

'I was pregnant. I had a stomach pain. I was frightened.'

'I was just about to give birth. Someone was trying to make me do something.'

A 29-year-old single girl with no children:

'I was pregnant. I had a little boy. I couldn't get used to him. He never cried or screamed. He was quite nice but he didn't seem normal.'

Some patients have dreams which are negative and

destructive, which is usually a bad sign, indicating that the therapy is not progressing well. It may indicate that the patient is about to break off treatment. Here are examples from two patients:

A 24-year-old recently-married woman consulted me. She was frigid and hated her father. Her mother was an Irish Catholic. She told me:

'I was having a baby. There was nobody about. I delivered the baby myself. I cut the cord. It was a little object. People appeared, including my husband. The baby shrivelled.'

'I gave birth. The baby had the umbilical cord twisted round its neck.'

The other patient was a widow who hadn't any children:

'I was outside with an ex-nurse. I had a baby. It was illegitimate. I wanted to get rid of it, to kill it. I wrapped it up in a cabbage. The refuse men came to collect it. The baby's feet were sticking out. The men saw a hand and covered it up. The police came to arrest me. I denied it.'

Dreams often do, of course, like some novels and films, have several meanings simultaneously.

THREE

Feeding

Mammals are animals whose mothers feed their young with milk, from the mammary glands. All mammals are born with the sucking instinct. Human babies are no exception. Whether breast-fed or bottle-fed, the baby sucks. The mouth is an important sensory organ. As adults, some of us have not grown out of this oral stage of development. This is usually due to having had an emotionally-deprived childhood. Some people compensate by smoking (although there can be other reasons why people smoke), some over-eat, or chew gum or stick various things in their mouths. Some people never get off the bottle; they progress from milk to alcohol.

Most children suck their thumbs. There is no harm in this and eventually they grow out of it. Some parents may worry if their child goes on sucking his thumb unduly long. This probably reflects a problem in the parent rather than in the child. I once met a married woman with children. She still sucked her thumb on certain occasions. It didn't appear to bother her and it was certainly less harmful than smoking or drinking, and much cheaper. Some parents fret if their child still sucks his thumb when other children of the same age do not. The parents may feel that their child is backward. The parents' anxiety would do the damage, not the thumb-sucking.

It is quite common for some parents to worry as to

whether their child is eating enough. Feeding can become an obsession with some mothers. They feel that the more the child eats the better. Some parents insist that the child finish all the food on his plate. Sometimes this is tantamount to force-feeding.

One of my patients, a man in his twenties, who wanted to get on the training course, was having the treatment which is a prerequisite for all trainees. He had various problems, but he had a good response to therapy, especially to hypnosis. During one of the early sessions he told me this in hypnosis:

'Dad takes me downstairs for something to eat. He puts me in my chair. There is an awful lot on my plate. I eat and eat. Roast potato – baked beans . . . an awful lot . . . getting full up . . can't eat any more. Mum comes in. Tells me to eat up. I've already eaten . . . mountains . . . bloody hell . . . I can't eat all that . . . sod you! What do you think I am? A dustbin? Stupid old cow . . . I'm not going to eat . . . mountains of the bloody stuff . . . blimey . . . I'll explode . . . I'm not going to eat it you old cow . . . don't care if I sit here all fucking night . . . I'm not going to eat . . . I don't want to . . . I'm not going to eat it . . . is that clear? Why does she want me to eat it? Thank god she's taken the plate away. A sweet . . . I'll eat that . . . nice and sweet . . . jelly and ice-cream . . . I'll have some more . . . stuff it all night. I can't eat it all . . . bloody mountains of jelly . . . huge. (He laughs.) So huge I'll stand on a chair and jump in . . . she expects me to eat it . . . bloody mad . . . I'll jump into it. She's taken it away, thank god. (He laughs.) Cup of tea . . . another mountain-full . . . huge cup of tea . . . too much . . . like a swimming pool . . . keeps giving me tea . . . biscuits of every kind. I like biscuits but it's too much, all this food everywhere . . . nice, really nice, but too bloody much . . . sausages – potatoes . . . mountains of jelly . . . oceans of tea. Now sweets . . . wheelbarrow of sweets . . . Smarties coming out of my ears . . . food everywhere . . . I can't take any more.'

This recollection of the patient's childhood is a good example of how a parent can overfeed a child. It can reflect the parent's problem. Food can become a love-substitute. Parents who cannot love their children may feel guilty and may stuff them with food to compensate. Lack of love by a parent is one of the fundamental problems in a parent/child relationship. Many parents believe that they love their children when in fact the reverse is true. The deprived parent demands love from the child, using him like a pet animal. A reverse situation is set up, where the parent becomes the demanding child, instead of the loving parent.

Some children are made to feel guilty about food. They are told:

'Eat up all your food! Think of all the people starving in Africa.'

This kind of nonsensical statement can confuse children as well as instil guilt. Some children may in turn use feeding to serve their own ends. Refusing to eat can be a way of showing feelings. I once knew a small boy who virtually refused to eat at home but when friends asked him out to tea he had no difficulty in eating. Away from his parents he seemed to have no feeding problems.

Some children, usually girls, develop anorexia in their teens. They can lose a frightening amount of weight. This can be a worry to their parents. Not only can this be vengeance against their parents, but a way of getting attention. Other children, when they are older, may put on weight and worry about their figure. Again, this applies mainly to girls, many of whom go on continual diets.

Some people are compulsive eaters, who, despite their conscious wish to lose weight, cannot stop overeating. A girl in her early twenties came to see me because she was overweight. She said she was a compulsive eater. She would go into a baker's shop and buy cakes which she would consume in the street. Then into the next bakery and do the same. When she could eat no more, she went home and vomited.

There are other reasons why people overeat. Women may (unconsciously) want to make themselves unattractive; men may want to look bigger and stronger. Some people may want to be overweight to be protected against the world. A fortress of fat.

One female patient told me:

'Having a layer of fat is a physical cage.'

Another female patient told me:

'Being overweight keeps men at bay. I feel so masculine when I'm overweight. Not feminine at all. Big and butch.'

A 26-year-old unmarried girl came to see me to lose weight. She was almost two stone overweight. She admitted:

'Deep down I don't want to lose weight. I'm happy outside but worry inside. I feel safe, protected by fat.'

As a child, her mother used to make her eat, saying:

'Eat your food – people are starving in Africa. Waste not, want not.'

I find that most patients who consult me for being overweight are women. Perhaps they are more concerned than men are about their looks and their figure.

Or it could be that their neuroses manifest themselves more this way. In virtually all patients I see with a weight problem, there is a sexual problem.

Another overweight female told me:

'Maybe I have a masculine side. When I'm overweight I feel masculine.' Her mother had told her that she wished she'd had all boys. Girls brought nothing but trouble.

One young attractive-looking female patient who was overweight also had sex problems:

'Being overweight is a way out of things I don't want to do. It's a safeguard against men. They'll ignore me if I'm overweight.'

Some people are unaware of their unconscious feelings regarding their weight. One such patient came to see me as she was grossly overweight, which was of great concern to her. Yet, despite her conscious wishes, she did not want to lose weight, which was made apparent by a Freudian slip. She said in one session:

'Being fat is attractive . . . I mean unattractive.'

She admitted that she lost weight when she had no boyfriend, yet put on weight when she did have one. She asked, getting a glimmer of insight:

'Am I unconsciously putting men off?'

Cannibalism is associated with primitive tribes, and is regarded by most people as a barbarous custom. Yet could there be vestiges of cannibalism in all of us? There have been cases of humans eating humans in recent times.

In 1972 an Uruguayan Air Force plane, chartered by a rugby team, crashed in the Andes, with a complement of forty-five passengers and crew. Ten weeks later sixteen survivors were rescued. They had survived by eating the corpses of their dead companions.

More recently, in 1981, a Japanese student, studying in Paris, shot his Dutch girlfriend when she wouldn't have sex with him. He cut her up, keeping various pieces in a refrigerator. He told the police he ate part of her: he had always wanted to eat a young woman.

Can cannibalism be directly connected with sucking at the breast? One patient I treated had a good response to hypnosis, which I used mostly at the beginning of his therapy. He usually regressed to childhood in hypnosis, remembering what happened as well as his emotional states. At one session he told me his feelings towards his mother and her breast, an important subject to a baby:

'I'm biting something . . . chewing . . . bite harder . . . bite and tear a breast . . . distance . . . not close enough. Bottle . . . chewing on rubber teat . . . breast . . . can't have it . . . what I'm chewing not what I want . . . like being thirsty with no water. This thing put in my mouth . . . all I can do is chew it . . . longing for something I can't get. Keep chewing this bloody rubber thing (the patient starts crying) . . . not going to get there. Want to suck and put my head between the breasts . . . not possible . . . have to stay at this distance. Bite . . . bite what I get . . . resigned to it now . . . take what I can get from bottle. Breasts further and further in distance . . . resigned to bottle. Everything out of reach.

'Going beyond the breasts . . . the whole of me . . . whole body . . . wants to be next to her body . . . locked in embrace . . . can't . . . beyond me . . . not there . . . want it, can't have it . . . want it! want it! can't have it . . . struggle for a tit. Can't let myself go . . . feel weak . . . beyond me . . . mother's image will always be out of reach . . . let feelings pour over me.'

Babies often try to bite their mother's breast.

One patient told me that she used to be a vegetarian some years previously, but that she now enjoyed eating meat. When she had a T-bone steak she couldn't help thinking that it looked like somebody's buttocks. 'I feel I'm eating somebody's body,' she said.

Another patient, a young female, had cannibalistic fantasies. She told me:

'I love eating raw meat. It's like eating a man's cock. It's not the taste I like, it's the texture. It's weird.'

Defecating
At the other end of the baby, waste matter is excreted. This is another sensitive area where problems may arise. At first the baby is incontinent. He lets go when he feels like it and, providing he's wearing a nappy, it's easily dealt with. There eventually comes a stage when the baby is toilet trained. With training, the baby sooner or later adapts to a routine. This can be an easy matter or a difficult one. The natural desire is to defecate at will. But the baby is conditioned to defecate at certain times and in certain places. The ease of training depends much on the relationship the baby has with his parents, especially the mother. The better the relationship, the easier the training. The child is co-operative. On the other hand, if the relationship is bad, the child may use toilet training as a weapon against mother or father or both. Children can show resentment and seek attention by not shitting. After all, what better way to get attention from an uninterested mother than to fail to release your shit and getting her all worked up? Some mothers don't like shit. It's dirty, smelly, and some women might find it difficult to get

used to changing and washing nappies. This might make some mothers try to encourage toilet training as early as possible, probably before the baby is ready for it.

Babies who hold back their shit and don't co-operate will suffer from constipation and may become stubborn and mean. This holding-back may also express itself in the inability to be loving.

Bed-wetting is a fairly common problem among children who are emotionally disturbed. Although this can often be cured by one of various mechanical gadgets, it is usually a symptom of an underlying problem and should be treated as such. One patient told me:

'I had an inferiority complex when I started off in life. I used to wet my bed until I was 25 years old. I bought a contraption which enabled me to stop in six months. Drinking bore no relationship. I used to wet my bed in my sleep, without waking.'

Shitting into underwear also happens with disturbed children. Parents should be aware of these symptoms and try and find out what is disturbing the child.

Sometimes, cleanliness is overstressed by the parents, which is a reflection of some inadequacy in them, not the child. Over-cleanliness is usually associated with repressed anal wishes. Many repressed (and overt) homosexuals are over-clean. I can remember one homosexual patient I treated who always drew out new notes from the bank to pay me.

Even today, in our more liberated society, shitting is still an embarrassing function for many, and shielded by euphemisms. In Britain we are still very strict about segregating men and women's lavatories, while in some other European countries it's common for men and women to share the same facilities.

Babies and children explore themselves. As a species we are curious. Shit is to be felt and explored. This isn't always allowed by parents. If touching shit is not acceptable to a parent, the child can always be encouraged to play with mud or plasticine which have much the same appearance and plasticity as shit.

Many people regard shit as dirty and, like sex and aggression, they feel that it is something that should not be brought out into the open. If this attitude is held by a parent it will inevitably affect the child in some way. Some institutions, such as boarding schools and hospitals, used to, and many probably still do, insist that you shit every day.

In my preparatory school, we were asked every day if we'd had 'a movement' the day before. If the answer was 'no' a laxative was administered by the matron. Not surprisingly, some boys didn't tell the truth.

FOUR

Sex
Since the beginning of our existence, sex has been of prime concern to man. It's a basic instinct which is essential for the species to reproduce and survive. Man reproduces sexually, the sexual urge being one of the strongest instincts we possess. The sperm from the male are injected, through the penis, into the female's vagina. Millions of sperm are released at a time. A teaspoonful of semen contains about 300 million sperm. The sperm then swim up through the womb and along one of the fallopian tubes to where the released egg is travelling down. Only one sperm completely penetrates the egg. A new life then develops, taking genes from both parents.

Our physical traits, and probably some of our mental traits, which we inherit from our parents, are determined by the combination of genes. The number we possess is uncertain, but it is somewhere between 2,000 and 50,000. If we assume that we inherit 10,000 from each parent, we possess 10,000 pairs, as each gene from one parent pairs up with a gene from the opposite parent. These genes are contained in chromosomes, 23 from each parent, making 46 in all. The potential variability of this selection is almost infinite. Our sex is determined by the combination of the sex chromosomes.

The sex-life of most species is confined to a particular period or to a particular cycle. Climate and seasons usually determine production of the young, spring being the obvious time to reproduce, when the weather is warm and there is plenty of food about. It also gives the young six months to grow and fatten before the next winter. The human race is different. People can copulate at any time and if the woman happens to be ovulating she can become pregnant irrespective of climate or conditions. Man is highly sexed, with the largest penis of the primates. A woman normally produces one child at a time. Producing more than one child at a time does occur occasionally: twins, of which a quarter are identical, occur in about one birth in ninety. Some women, for various reasons, are unable to become pregnant. Sometimes a fertility drug is given, with amazing results. In August 1979, an Italian mother, Mrs Pasqualina Chianese, aged 29, gave birth to octuplets. She had been taking a fertility drug.

I have heard of cases where a married couple have been unable to produce any children. Having adopted a child, the wife then becomes pregnant. This happened to a patient of mine, even before she adopted a child. She told me:

'My inability to conceive may have been psychological. I'd been trying to get pregnant for six years. We eventually decided to adopt a child. I became pregnant – that same month. I became very calm once I'd decided to adopt.'

Although sex is a natural instinct, in man it's largely governed by the mind. Virtually all sexual problems are emotional. A man may be impotent or a woman inorgasmic, but these are not physical problems; they are psychosexual problems. Social and parental attitudes are generally the causes of sexual difficulties. As a therapist I find many patients suffer from sexual problems, usually caused by repressed feelings. In fact if there is an emotional problem there's usually a sexual problem.

Sex dominates a large part of our lives, determining much of what we do even if we are not aware of it. When and where do our first sexual feelings start? Like much else, with our parents. After the mouth and the anus, the genitals are the third important sensitive area. All children have sexual feelings even though they may not become manifest until puberty. It has been known for baby boys to have erections at birth; certainly boys can get erections and girls can get orgasms before puberty, and children have been known to copulate before puberty. Many parents like to believe that children are sexually innocent. This belief in purity and innocence can often inhibit children in sexual matters. Far more harm is done by attempts to shield children from sex than by exposing them to it.

If we remember that we are an inquisitive species, it is not surprising that children want to know why the opposite sex is different and in what way. Children often inspect each others' genitals, making comparisons, often to the alarm of their 'respectable' parents. These comparisons lead to the big question in the child's mind: 'Why don't girls have a penis?' A child's logic will come up with the answer that girls have lost their penis in some way. This may lead to penis-envy in girls and fear of castration in boys.

A 32-year-old female patient told me this dream:

'There was a little girl. She was not quite normal. She wanted to have a pee and pulled up her dress. She had a penis.'

Another young patient was quite aware of her penis-envy:

'When I was much younger I used to envy my brother. He had a penis. I used to wish I had one. I can remember envying him for that reason.'

Another young married female told me this:

'As a little girl I thought I was a boy. Then I changed. Had my penis disappeared inside me? I'm continually having doctors looking up my cunt. I have a fantasy of having a penis. Only me and my mother know about it. I was supposed to be a boy. I was called William before I was born.

'A little girl at my school had similar thoughts. I asked her why. She said the doctor did it. She used to have a penis. "When?" I asked her. When she was a boy, she said.'

Some female patients have inadvertently used expressions which denote their fears or wishes regarding their sexual role. One divorcee said:

'My parents cut off any normal growth.'

Another female patient said:

'I feel my car is a physical extension of me. When I had to leave it at the garage for a week, it felt as if something had been cut off.'

Sometimes dreams can be illuminating. One female patient told me this dream:

'I went to the breast clinic. The nurse showed me straight in. There was a big black man, rough looking. I lay on a bed. The X-ray machine came down. I had my hand over a breast. I couldn't pull it away. Eventually I managed. A finger showed a shadow on the X-ray.'

Castration fears can be very strong in men and it has been known for some men, usually through feelings of guilt, to castrate themselves. Vasectomy is a comparatively new form of contraception and it has been found that some men enjoy a morbid satisfaction from this operation. Some may regard it as a safe form of castration. It's estimated that, every year, 100,000 men in Britain have vasectomies. There is no hard evidence that there are harmful long-term effects, but there is no doubt that the male sperm, denied their normal outlet, seep into the bloodstream and antibodies are formed. Some people fear this might be harmful.

A child's love and sex feelings towards its parents will determine its feelings to people in adult life. A mother will always be the first love, symbolised by the breast. Later, the father, whose love is symbolised by the penis. Both parents are essential to a child. Should one or both parents be absent, it can spell trouble for the child. Unfortunately, many parents get divorced, separate or die. Many fathers are away from home a lot; some have to be away on business or are in the services and are posted away from home. Some fathers who commute great distances to and from work, leaving before the children are up and returning after they're in bed, only see their children at week-ends. An absent parent leaves an emotional gap which is usually filled in some neurotic manner. An absent father may cause his son's homosexual feelings to become predominant to make up for the lack of relationship between father and son. A girl, if she is deprived of a father, may develop an intense hatred of men. Some girls looking for a father-figure marry an older man or get involved with married men. It is less likely for a mother to be absent than a father but if she is this may cause her son to hate women and her daughter to become homosexual.

Parental sexual attitudes are a great influence on a child's sexual development, both physically and mentally. I have found that girls are affected more than boys, probably because many parents feel that their daughters need protecting and consequently instil fears and fallacies in their children. Or the parents, because of their own repressions, may ignore the sexual education of their daughters completely.

Here are some things patients have told me.

A 40-year-old married woman with two children:

'I find it difficult to talk about sex. I would rather do it than talk about it. When I was 11 years old my mother told me that if I ever got into trouble, if I ever missed a period, to let her know. I didn't even know what a period was.'

An 18-year-old girl student:

'When I first turned into a woman, when I was 12 or 13 years old, I was ashamed of myself. I didn't like the look of myself.'

Another patient, a 29-year-old married woman, always sat in the chair during her sessions. She said:

'I don't like lying on the couch. It has associations with sex. That disturbs me. I don't like admitting to sex problems.'

She then started crying, releasing pent-up feelings.

A 56-year-old French widow told me:

'I'm not an animal. I'm above animals, civilized. Sex was taboo in my family. I was brought up a Catholic.'

Some young people are very ignorant about sex, even today. Sometimes they can be told extraordinary things which they believe. One young patient, a girl in her teens, said:

'My brother told me that you can get pregnant by kissing. When I was younger I didn't want to get too close to my boyfriend in case I got pregnant.'

An Irish woman patient told me her father was very sexually repressed, with incestuous feelings.

'I thought once that my father was going to make

love to me. It was the night he beat me up in the bathroom. I found him embarrassing to be with.'

A young female patient told me about her parents:

'When I first masturbated I was about nine years old. My mother was annoyed. She told me off. We were at grandma's house. My brother and I were exposing our bodies. Father discovered us. He gave my brother the tanning of his life. I hid under the bed. He didn't find me for hours.'

Incest taboo

The incest taboo has been in existence a long time. A father/daughter, mother/son or brother/sister union is illegal. So are other marriages between near relatives. The Marriage (Enabling) Act 1960 forbids the marriage of twenty categories of near relatives. Congenital malformations may occur if the union of near relatives produces offspring. All humans carry potentially harmful recessive genes which may cause deformities if both parents possess the same harmful genes. The nearer the relationship between the parents, the greater the chance of a genetic mischance. A daughter, for example, will inherit half her genes from her father. If their union produces a child, there is a strong mathematic possibility of the child inheriting a combination of harmful recessive genes, as both parents would have at least half their genes in common.

There have been notable exceptions to the incest taboo in the past. Royalty in Ancient Egypt and the Incas in Peru actively encouraged inbreeding, as did certain rulers in Africa. Although inbreeding was encouraged in certain of these ruling classes, no such matings were permitted to the general public.

The incest taboo, although there are sound reasons for its existence, has influenced social attitudes and in some cases has helped to develop excessive sexual taboos within family relationships. This in turn has had the effect of causing some parents to repress their sexual feelings towards their children.

Puberty is a time when children become manifestly sexual. Girls start menstruating and their breasts develop. Boys start getting erections and grow beards. The cuddly child becomes a sexually active teenager. A father of a well-developed, attractive girl of 14 or 15 might find it embarrassing to have any physical contact with her and may withdraw his love. Equally, a mother might be embarrassed by her son getting erections. One of my patients told me that her father lost interest in her when she reached the age of puberty. This is the very time when a girl becomes sexually aware and most needs her father's affection. Boys also need their mother's affection at puberty.

Sometimes these repressed incestuous feelings are released in dreams. One female patient who had been married and had five children told me this dream:

'I was making love to my son. He was underneath me.'

Another patient, a divorced woman, told me this dream:

'I took all my clothes off and walked up the Earls Court Road. I went into the police station. I was gang-banged by the policemen. I enjoyed it. I was also fucked from behind.'

Policemen are authority-figures, and patients often use them as father-substitutes in dreams.

A 30-year-old bachelor told me this dream:

'I was in bed. Mum was sitting on the bed. She was

going all strange. She was drunk or stoned. She was trying to seduce me. I was trying to calm her down. She was telling me she needed screwing. I thought she was going round the bend.'

Incestuous wishes are not restricted to heterosexual feelings: they can also take the form of homosexual feelings.

A 29-year-old Swedish patient, an unmarried girl, told me this lesbian dream:

'Me and mother were fucking. I also saw her masturbate. She had a penis. She was very skilled. Sometimes she had the penis, sometimes I did.'

Some patients are quite aware of their incestuous feelings or their parents' incestuous feelings. One young girl patient told me:

'The first man I was ever attracted to looked like my father. I was 8 years old.'

She also told me a dream:

'I was with my brother. He was much older, more like a man. We were having sex. He was on top of me.'

Freudian slips sometimes express inner desires. One patient, a bachelor, referred to his mother as 'my woman' by mistake. He had a mother-fixation and found it very difficult to form relationships with women.

Another patient, a young girl, one of two children, disclosed her feelings towards her brother. She said:

'I went to see my parents over the weekend. My brother was there with his sister – I mean his wife.'

If a child feels unloved, he may, in adult life, have difficulty in loving – or in accepting love.

Many parents, because of their emotional problems, are unable to love their children. Some parents repress any feelings of love, or any manifestation of it, toward their children, because they fear that these feelings would be accompanied by incestuous desires. Fear of incestuous feelings surfacing can also cause parents to make their children feel guilty about sex.

Incestuous feelings are often the cause of possessiveness. This, not just local or religious custom, can cause parents to insist on themselves making the choice of spouse for their children (and perhaps finding no prospective spouse suitable), or regarding the virginity of their daughters, or sons, as a prized possession.

One reason why some parents make their children feel guilty about having a sexual relationship with anyone is jealousy. Many people grow up feeling that they have to be faithful to their parents. There are men who live with one of their parents until the parent dies. Some daughters devote their whole lives to looking after one of their parents. In France, there is an expression 'Un baton de vieillesse' – a prop for old age. In some families in France it's considered the duty of the youngest daughter to look after her parents in their old age. One elderly French patient of mine, whose father was dead, told me that her youngest sister was still looking after her mother, who was 82 years old. The daughter had no chance of living a life of her own.

Sexual feelings between members of a family are, of course, normal. But many of my patients who find that they have sexual feelings toward their parents have difficulty in accepting these feelings.

Homosexuality
Your sex is determined at conception. Sex genes from the female, contained in the X chromosome, combine with sex genes from the male, contained in the X or Y

chromosome, producing a girl (XX) or a boy (XY). This cannot be altered. You are either a boy or a girl. There have been only 303 true hermaphrodites recorded in medical history. These are the result of freak chances when genes combine incorrectly.

Male embryos develop a penis and testicles, while female embryos develop a vagina, womb and ovaries. Hormones which are released from the endocrine glands in the body give you your male or female secondary characteristics. This takes place at puberty, when hormones influence changes in the body. In males, hair grows on the face and on the pubic area, the voice breaks and frequent erections occur which often lead to ejaculation. Girls at puberty find their breasts enlarging and pubic hair growing. They begin to menstruate. They also develop the 'female form', rounder and softer than the body of the male.

The human male, as virtually all males of other species of animals, is biologically more aggressive than the human female. As children are sexual, even if they are not aware of it, it would logically follow that boys will be of a more aggressive nature than girls. I would consider it natural for boys to be attracted to play with more aggressive toys, such as soldiers, while girls would be attracted to more passive toys, such as dolls. Some people believe that as children are normally given toys according to their sex, this could be indoctrination, not a natural choice by the child. But there's no reason why children should not be given toys usual for their sex, provided they are allowed to choose, when they want to do so, what toys are given to them and which toys they play with.

By nature, males are aggressive, while females are passive. These are the sexual roles, although at the same time there is no dividing line down the middle. Females do produce male hormones as males produce female hormones, but there is always a preponderance of one sexual hormone or the other, according to our sex, which gives us our sexual features and attitudes.

At the same time men can be passive, just as women are sometimes aggressive. It is important to remember this when dealing with sexual abnormalities, particularly the most common, homosexuality. Sometimes the sexual positions between lovers may be reversed, the woman being on top, taking the dominant role, while the man is passive. This is not unnatural and should not be considered as a sign of homosexuality. It can add stimulus to sex life.

Some homosexuals (men and women) consider that nature has played them a nasty trick: a man's mind in a woman's body or vice-versa. This is a rationalisation which conveniently explains their behaviour, but there is no truth in it. Homosexuality is a mental problem, not a physical one, caused by a faulty parent/child relationship. A child of either sex may become a homosexual through having a dominant mother and a passive father, or through a parent being absent, or through having an unloving relationship with one or both parents.

To date, I have been consulted by about twenty male homosexuals, that is men who are practising homosexuals, who have no sexual interest in women and have no wish to change. They could be considered 100% homosexual. They all had fathers who either didn't like children, were away a lot, died when the patient was young, or were weak, ineffectual men. Out of these twenty patients, only four proceeded with treatment, one coming for about a year. Some changed their sexual outlook to some extent, and all benefitted in other ways. Less anxiety was the main improvement. They felt more relaxed, finding it easier to get on with people. Lack of communication with their fathers was a trait common to these patients.

I have been consulted by only two or three female homosexuals, none of whom embarked on therapy. This may be because female homosexuals have a deep-seated resentment towards their fathers. As I am a male therapist, they would see me as their hated father. A male homosexual may find it easier to see a male therapist, as he would probably have less of a negative transference than would a lesbian. One male homosexual patient of mine had a very positive transference and made good progress.

One cause, probably the main cause, of male homosexuality, is lack of love from the father. Many men, because they are emotionally crippled (and probably have repressed incestuous wishes), are unable to express any love or tenderness towards their sons.

One male homosexual patient told me:

'My father's attitude was arrogant. I've been wanting a man's love as a result of that. My father didn't love me. I want to be accepted.'

Another patient with homosexual problems told me of his hostility towards his father:

'I hated my father when I was living at home. I resented him. He was incapable of showing any emotion. I only got a response by making him angry. He only kissed me once – when I got married.'

Absent or dead fathers have much the same effect on their sons. A 22-year-old male homosexual came to see me because he suffered from nervousness. He told me at the consultation that when he was seven years old his father died. In addition, the father had been an alcoholic, and away from home a lot, having been in the Merchant Navy. During one of his sessions the patient told me:

'I didn't want people at college to know I was homosexual. I was looking for a father-figure in older men. Looking for security.'

At another session he told me:

'I was lying on my bed with George, watching television. I had the feeling of being back with my father. They were very alike.'

Unloving or absent fathers can confuse the child's idea of his or her sexual role. Homosexuals, both male and female, whatever their outward behaviour, are very hostile people, and as patients I have found that they are very difficult to treat. I have not known of a committed homosexual who has accepted his or her sexual role to have become heterosexual as a result of therapy. Not that they want to change; they usually come for treatment for some other affliction. But a good therapist treats the whole personality, not isolated symptoms. Psychological problems are usually interrelated anyway.

Patients that I have helped to recover from their homosexuality have been ones who were 'pseudo-bisexuals', and did not want to be homosexual. In other words they had lapses when they indulged in homosexual activity but wished they didn't. Again, my experience has been restricted to males, but I have no reason to believe that the same would not apply to females.

A 21-year-old bachelor, who was a social worker, came to see me because he had various problems he wanted to sort out. One problem was that he was unable to make love to a woman. He always lost his erection as he was entering his partner. On the other hand he had no problems in having sex with men, although this made him feel guilty. He was also worried about having superfluous hair on his body. This had bothered him since he was 10 years old. He was intelligent and articulate, but also very aggressive. He was born in India after his father had come to England to settle. The patient did not see his father until he was seven years old. He did not get on with him, having rows with him all the time. He was his mother's favourite son, which he felt led her to spoiling him. He also had a fantasy that they weren't his real parents. He was not an easy patient to deal with, due to his outbursts of aggressive behaviour, but with perseverance he gradually sorted out his sexual problems. He eventually got engaged to be married, and soon after broke off from treatment. This was against my professional advice, as he still had a number of problems to sort out. He had attended 172 sessions over three years, coming on a regular basis. Two years later, after I had contacted him, he wrote to me saying, among other things:

'I am happy to inform you that since leaving therapy I have made much progress in accepting myself as I am – warts and all!

'My analysis has helped me in my work, where sensitivity and insight into myself can be adequately translated to meet and perceive client need, while avoiding some of the major blindspots so prevalent in this "helping" profession.

'In terms of my own personal needs, psychotherapy has been quite invaluable.

'I have been happily married for two years now. Helen and I are extremely close and very much in love.'

Another young man, 21 years old, consulted me because he thought he was bisexual. He said that he fancied men in the street but did not like himself for it. He indulged in homosexual experiences, especially after he'd been drinking. It made him feel sick afterwards, and the problem was getting worse, which frightened him. His father had died when the patient was 13 years old, leaving him to be brought up by his mother, and two older brothers who bullied him. He attended therapy three times a week for about two months, after which he said that he was all right and broke off treatment against my advice. He had responded well to therapy, making good progress, but he still hadn't resolved all his problems. About a year later I happened to meet him socially and, unsolicited, he told me how much he had gained from therapy. He said he only had homosexual escapades once every six months instead of weekly. He also intended to resume treatment to sort out his problem completely.

Many people repress their homosexual tendencies, and many of my patients discovered, sometimes as a shock, that they had homosexual feelings. I have found that, among my patients, repressed homosexuality is more apparent among males than females. This may be due to men being more afraid of homosexual feelings and finding them more difficult to accept. Many males are brought up to be tough and manly, not showing any female traits. Women perhaps are less afraid of homosexual feelings and are not hindered by such a strong homosexual taboo as men can be.

If there are any repressed homosexual feelings in patients, these feelings will eventually come out in therapy. If a patient is not ready to accept his homosexual tendencies, the therapist should use his skill and judgement, steering the patient away from this realisation until he is able to accept it. Very often, patients stop treatment rather than face their homosexuality. One patient, at the consultation, told me that he'd had a homosexual experience once, after getting drunk. Once sober, this act had made him feel so guilty that he had attempted to commit suicide.

One question I always ask a prospective patient is: 'Have you ever had any homosexual experiences?' Some say they have had, when young or when at school, while others are quite shocked, saying that homosexuality disgusts them. This last reaction comes mostly from male patients.

According to Kinsey, 40% of adult American men, and 13% of women, had experienced homosexual contact to point of orgasm. If this is correct, homosexuality is probably more common than most of us realise or would like to believe.

Some people gratify their repressed homosexual urges in various ways, some subtle, some less subtle. One way is to share a lover. Two men can feel sexually related (at an unconscious level) by using the same woman, while two women can feel this by using the same man.

One patient, a married woman of 40, told me she'd had a one-off affair with the local playboy. She then went on to say:

'He then asked me to go with this other man. Why? I couldn't believe it.'

I have found that in many male patients, particularly the pushy, bossy types, homosexuality is strongly linked with feelings of paranoia. This could link up with a wish/fear to be attacked/raped by their father. I have found that homosexuals suffer from repressed aggression – aggression which they often project onto others. Sometimes they try to compensate by bullying and being pushy. This kind of patient is difficult to keep going, as there is so much stored-up hostility. Again, the more experienced and able the practitioner, the better the chances of a successful outcome.

Until fairly recently (1967), it was illegal in Britain for men to have a homosexual relationship, while women were not penalised for the same offence. Possibly this anomaly was brought about by the fact that men made the laws and must have been afraid of their own repressed homosexuality. The Criminal Law Amendment Act 1885 could put a man in jail for homosexual activities. Some people believe Queen Victoria struck out women from the Law before signing. If so, perhaps she could not accept the idea of lesbianism. In the United Kingdom, consenting adults over 21 are allowed to practise homosexuality in private.

Impotence
Sexual impotence in men can be a debilitating and embarrassing symptom which not only prevents any chance of sexual intercourse, but can lead to grave anxiety and loss of confidence. For a man to admit that he cannot get an erection can be a humiliating experience.

There can be many reasons why a man fails to attain an erection. One cause can be a deep-seated unconscious fear that his penis might get damaged or cut off if he enters a woman. If, as a child, he was made to feel guilty about his sexual feelings towards his mother, it could result in him avoiding sex altogether or in not being able to get an erection with a woman. Many men who are impotent are able to masturbate, or have a sexual relationship with another man, but when in contact with a woman they fail completely. Fear of castration is a fairly common symptom among men, even those who are able to get an erection and enter a woman.

Sexual guilt in men can be caused by a mother with repressed sexual feelings. It can also be caused by a father's jealousy regarding his son's sexual feelings towards his mother. Many men who are riddled with sexual guilt have very strong wish/fear feelings regarding castration.

Another reason for a man failing to get an erection, or losing it on entering a woman, can be a deep hatred of all women, stemming from having an unloving mother. After all, why give a woman pleasure by fucking her, if you see her, unconsciously, as your hated mother? This hatred of women can also be expressed by retarding ejaculation or not ejaculating at all while fucking. This could be an unconscious holding-back, as with a woman who is inorgasmic. Hatred of women can also be expressed by ejaculating prematurely, thus not giving the female partner a chance of getting an orgasm.

Impotence, retarded ejaculation and premature ejaculation often have common causes – causes which originate with the parent/child relationship. Sometimes the symptoms are severe, sometimes not. The less severe the symptom, the easier to correct the problem.

The following case illustrates clearly some of the causes of impotence, causes which could also apply to the other problems I have mentioned concerning men's sexuality.

This case concerns a man of 24 who came to see me because he was impotent and thought that hypnosis would help him overcome this problem. He said that he'd not sought help previously because he was too embarrassed to mention his problem to anybody. He'd once had sex with a woman when he was in his teens, but at the age of 19 he became impotent. He also bit his nails and lacked confidence.

He told me that his father was overbearing, stubborn and had a bad temper, which had made the patient scared of him. The patient was closer to his mother, but they didn't have much in common. I agreed to see him twice a week. At the beginning of the therapy, his response wasn't good; he didn't remember his dreams and he had a poor response to hypnosis. But as therapy progressed his response improved. On his second visit, in hypnosis, he said:

'My mother made me feel guilty about sex when I was a kid. I was furtive about reading girlie magazines. I used to tear them up and get rid of them. I rarely took girls home. Mother told me to ditch my girl. She cried: "You don't love your Mum any more!"'

On his next visit, in hypnosis:

'I feel more confident.

'First time I made love – sounds stupid – it was to an older woman, 40 years old. She was married to an older man, 60 years old, who drank. I was 16 years old, still wet behind the ears. I went round to her house. Went to the bedroom. I was frightened the husband might come back. Also that my parents might find out. Association of women and mother. Mother wouldn't approve. The woman was hard outside, soft inside. She was upset – not satisfied. My brother is always in trouble. When I was 11 years old I shoplifted some sweets.'

At the next session he told me;

'My parents' attitudes annoy me. Father thinks it's more manly to fight. It was being sissy to read books and study. When I was three he joined the army to fight in Korea. He was away three years. He's incapable of thinking for himself. Mother leads him.'

This patient had a tendency to be late for his sessions, which is usually a sign of hostility. But he started to remember his dreams. In one of them, his mother fell in front of a car. He told me:

'When I was ten years old I used to play with girls of my age. We used to look at and touch each others' genitals. My parents taunted me, saying I was talking to girls too much. My parents laughed at me, especially my father.'

At the following session, in hypnosis:

'I felt I was competing with father for mother. My brother would compete on the same terms. I couldn't, I can't do manual things. I never compete – I pull out of competitions. I'd fail trying to fight father and brother. My brother is younger. He'd start a fight and I'd get the blame. If I thought of making love to girls, I felt I would be competing with past lovers.'

At the next session he said he'd been home on Sunday and found he'd got on much better with his parents – better than he had for ages. He also felt more confident and was looking for another job. At the following session he told me:

'Mother frowned on sex. When I was 17 I liked a girl. Mother made snide remarks.

'When I was five years old I went to a party. I had a lot to eat and drink. I went to the toilet three times. I was afraid to ask again. I defecated in my trousers.

59

Toilet training – it was unclean to be constipated.'

At the next session:

'I'm scared of scissors. Might cut my genitals off. Afraid of losing my manhood.

'Father away a long time. When he came back, he was a stranger. I'm frightened of coming here.'

At the following session he said he resented more and more coming for therapy. He was annoyed with himself and with me. He felt that women were more dominant. They manipulated men. He felt he wasn't dominant enough.

At this point in therapy he told me that he no longer got stomach upsets the night before coming for therapy. He continued:

'I have a fear of being made to look a fool. Being ridiculed by girls. My parents laughed at me instead of correcting. I felt very guilty at my first experience of sex as a child. Mother was quick to point out all that is rude, dirty or nasty. They couldn't cope with kids. They weren't much use – they repressed everything. I was the oldest – a guinea-pig. My three-year-old sister had no knickers on. She was playing with herself. Father smacked her.'

By now he had found a girlfriend, but he was jealous, especially as she had a lot of friends.

Some sessions later he told me that he felt less shy and more confident but his impotence was still a problem. He didn't like talking about it. He added that he had masturbated a lot when younger. He felt guilty about it, believing it made you blind and impotent. He didn't want his parents to know that he masturbated. He had a revulsion for female genitals. 'They don't look or smell nice.' He wondered why he was afraid of putting his penis in.

At the next session he said he'd seen some blue films.

'How could good-looking girls do those kind of things?'

By now his response to hypnosis was much better, with both his arms going up by suggestion, something he hadn't done previously. He was still arriving late for his sessions, finding various excuses for being late. He had also broken up with his girlfriend. 'Sexual problems,' he said. He found her too demanding and resented that she depended so much on her parents.

Two sessions later he reported that he'd made love twice. It was all right. Quite spontaneous. 'I feel good. A load off my shoulders. I don't feel like an outcast.'

He was finding that he was wanting sex more and more. Also that he was finding it easier to form relationships, and was being attracted to younger girls.

He was quite frightened of being dominated by women. 'Mother dominated father. She's mentally superior. Father's pathetic.'

At this point he terminated therapy, against my advice. He had overcome his impotence, but he hadn't resolved his other problems, especially his hostile feelings which he had, basically, towards his father. This probably precipitated his termination of therapy, as he transferred his hostility to me and, as soon as his presenting symptom was resolved, he didn't want to proceed any further. He'd attended 25 sessions over five months.

I have found that male sexual problems such as impotence, retarded ejaculation and premature ejaculation can be resolved fairly rapidly. Perhaps because the problem manifests itself in a physical symptom, it indicates that it's not as deep-seated as other sexual problems. Sexual problems which manifest themselves in sexual attitudes are more difficult to remove, and may take a long time.

Orgasmic inability
Among my patients I have found that impotence in men is not nearly as common as inorgasm in women. Whether this is a correct reflection of the facts in general, in that inorgasm in women is far more common than impotence in men, or whether men are less likely to admit they are impotent and seek help, I'm not certain.

Orgasmic inability in women can be a serious symptom but, unlike impotence, which prevents a man from having sex, it doesn't prevent a woman from performing the sexual act. Many women don't admit they can't get an orgasm, sometimes feigning a climax to appear quite normal to their sexual partners.

Orgasmic inability is a symptom which affects most of the female patients who consult me. I have found that all these patients had a bad relationship, or no relationship at all, with their fathers. These patients all had difficulties in forming loving relationships with a man, usually choosing a man who is totally unsuitable, at the same time complaining about their man, saying how unloving he is and how bad the relationship is.

I have found that, in virtually all these cases, orgasmic inability is the last symptom to be resolved. This is not surprising, as many of women's feelings towards men are centred around the genitals. By not having an orgasm the woman could be holding back, not giving herself to her sex partner. She could be showing the man that he's not good enough, that he's not a good lover, not being able to satisfy her.

However, occasionally one comes across a patient who recovers fairly quickly from her inability to have orgasms. One such patient was a girl of 26 who came from Sweden. She had lived in England for eight years. Her presenting symptoms were smoking, nervousness, insecurity and blushing. She was also frightened of becoming an alcoholic as she used wine as a tranquilliser. She also told me that at the age of 14 she had developed terrible acne on her face which had left unsightly scars down one side.

She had been living with her boyfriend for six years and, although they got on well, she was unable to get an orgasm. She told me that her father had been a successful businessman who used to be away from home a lot. He had also been an alcoholic. When the patient was 10 years old, he died in a fire caused by his lighted cigarette. She got on well with her mother who she said had a strong and warm personality. (Later in therapy she realised that this had been a misconception. Her mother turned out to be a possessive and manipulative woman, using her children for her own ends.) There were three other children in the family, all older than the patient, none of them married.

I agreed to see the patient twice a week. She was co-operative as well as intelligent and articulate, making good progress. About four months later she reported:

'The other night I couldn't sleep. I was restless, feeling generally angry. I felt I wanted to fight someone; I had an excess of energy. John was asleep, but my tossing and turning woke him up. We started to have sex. I then had an orgasm very quickly. It was a very emotional experience; I was laughing and crying at the same time.'

After that she had no further problems with orgasms, but she thought it strange that she hadn't been able to experience one before.

Sex with animals
Humans having sex with animals does occur, but nowadays probably mainly in remote peasant communities. In Argentina, I once heard of a cavalry officer who used to disappear in the evenings; it was eventually discovered that he used to go to the stables and, using a stool, fuck one of the mares. He was court-martialled.

However, many people have fantasies or dreams about having sex with animals.

I have found that some patients, usually women, have sexual feelings or fantasies towards animals. One French girl patient had a strong fantasy of a dog licking her cunt.

A 34-year-old female patient related this dream:

'I was having sexual intercourse with a pony.' She added that she owned the pony when she was 12 years old.

An unmarried girl of 22 came to see me. She had many problems, mainly feelings of guilt and anxiety. She was still a virgin. She told me:

'I had a problem of sex with animals about eight months ago, but I got over it. I went over to see James on Sunday. He has a little corgi. I had several thoughts about it. I was petting with James on the floor. I saw him as an animal.

'When I was eight or nine years old, the black labrador down the road pinned me up against a fence. Another time he got me in a sexual position. I couldn't get away.'

Another patient, a 26-year-old Irishman, came to see me because he had difficulty in forming sexual relationships with women. He told me this dream, which he found embarrassing to relate:

'I was doing funny things with a male dog. It was buggering me. It left something inside me. Afterwards I pulled something out. It was six inches long. It was the shape of the dog's penis.'

First sexual experiences can often leave a lasting impression, especially if they occur around puberty or earlier. In some cases they can become fixations and therapy is needed to resolve the problem.

Having or wanting sex with an animal can be appealing inasmuch as there is no emotional involvement. Some people are not able to become emotionally involved with a sex partner. Some men resort to prostitutes, and there are cases of men being able to get an erection only with a prostitute.

Improved sex life from an outside stimulus

Sometimes a new or different experience can help someone with sexual problems. Some people get married without gaining any sexual experience first. Later, they may regret it. They start wondering if their husband/wife is the same as other men/women. They may become curious and want to compare their spouse with other lovers.

One young married woman who came to see me said she was a virgin when she married, she had sex less than once a week and she was inorgasmic. She also found penetration painful. At the consultation she told me that the marriage was marvellous and that she got on very well with her husband. As the therapy progressed, she began to realise that her marriage wasn't the blissful state she liked to think it was. This was not surprising as her father was weak and emotionally cold. He was timid, yet had outbursts of anger. She said she wasn't able to talk to him. Her mother, she stated, didn't like men.

After a number of sessions, she told me that she was interested in a man at work. She was attracted to him and wanted to have sex, but felt very inhibited and didn't want to be unfaithful to her husband. (She had been brought up a Catholic.) She was sick the first time she went out with the new man. Eventually she started an affair with this man, with enormous benefits. She said that sex was now absolutely fantastic. She didn't get any pains and she also got orgasms. She felt she wasn't holding anything back with her lover, while she was with her husband. She didn't want to leave her husband and found that, after she had started her affair, she was getting on better with him. She thought that the affair would help her marriage.

Sometimes other outside influences such as sex magazines, or erotic stories, plays or films, may help sex life in a relationship. One male patient told me he took his girlfriend to see 'Belle de Jour', the erotic French film. That night, he said, they went wild in bed – 'we ripped the bedroom apart – we both let loose. I found myself again that night, it was a rediscovery.'

FIVE

Aggression

As I have already mentioned, we are aggressive animals by nature. Some people find this hard to accept, going to great lengths to avoid it or to try to prove that we, as humans, aren't aggressive by nature. Disciples of some analytic schools of thought, such as Adlerian or Jungian, don't believe that we as a race are naturally aggressive. This has much appeal to people who would rather avoid their aggressive feelings.

Animals are aggressive. They have to be, to survive. Predators are aggressive in killing and eating their prey. Animals also fight to preserve their territory. Even the timid rabbit will fight. Animals will also fight to ward off other males from their females. Females with young are very aggressive. I have seen a hen blackbird attack a cat which has come too close to her nest. Yet animals hardly ever kill for the sake of killing. A fox may go berserk in a chicken run and kill far more than it can eat, but usually animals only kill to eat or in order to defend their territory, their females or their young.

Most animals in a particular species live in groups or in pairs. In groups, one male is usually dominant. But not all animals are sociable. Robins and moles for instance only co-habit to mate, spending the rest of the time alone, defending their territory. Acting in groups, animals are better able to protect themselves. Some predators, such as lions and wolves, hunt in packs which are highly organised. Grouping is also beneficial in protecting territory.

Within groups, the animals establish a pecking order which enables all the individuals in the group to know how they stand in respect of the others. The strongest and most aggressive male is usually dominant, with the rest in a pecking order after him. The order can be disrupted if a stranger is admitted, although it is usually driven off or killed. Having a pecking order usually ensures that the offspring are fathered by the strongest male.

Humans also have a type of pecking order. We know roughly how we stand in respect of other people. Some of us are more dominant and aggressive than others. In any human group a hierarchy is soon set up. When people meet for the first time, quite often there is a period during which they assess each other. They may both be slightly defensive to begin with, testing each other out, to see how they stand in the social order.

As a race, we have removed ourselves so far from nature that we find it difficult to express openly our natural instincts, aggression in particular. When aggression does break out in a big way, such as in a world war, unthinkable atrocities are committed. In normal situations we are taught to obey the law which disallows killing. But if a war is declared, permission is given to kill. The Germans are a very obedient and law-conscious nation, but during the second world war unbelievably sadistic acts were committed by some of them.

Bad behaviour at football matches reflects the frustrated aggression that many youths suffer from. Fighting on the terraces is an outlet for many whose lives are boring and who are unable to express their aggression freely. If one is low down in the pecking order, there is not much to peck at.

Some people confuse aggression with anger. Aggression is an innate instinct which we all need in order to survive. Anger is normally a self-defence mechanism. You don't have to get angry to be aggressive, although the two often go together. Children get angry very easily, usually from frustration. A child wants and expects everything at once. This is not always possible and the child has to learn patience. Unfortunately, many parents don't bring up their children sufficiently well to be able to cope with their anger and frustration. Some parents spoil their children by giving them everything they want for the sake of peace and quiet, while others suppress their children who then are unable to express any feelings of anger or aggression.

It is not possible to have everything on demand. A child has to learn patience. When a baby doesn't get what it wants it has no hesitation in expressing anger and frustration, which can test the patience of the parents. With good upbringing, a child learns to be reasonable in its demands as well as to be patient.

We have two types of anger. One is the natural defensive anger necessary for survival when we are threatened. The other type of anger is the immature anger we associate with children. If the latter is still apparent in adult life it would indicate that there are feelings which have not been worked through with the parents. Providing children are allowed to express their feelings freely, within certain bounds, problems needn't arise later in life. Many parents don't allow their children to express their feelings sufficiently when necessary. Some parents are bullies, trying to compensate for their own lack of aggression by taking it out on their children. Or they may be frightened of their own aggression, not being able to express it and not allowing their children to, either.

What happens to aggression if it's suppressed? It will find outlets in other ways, quite often in physical symptoms. Many patients consult me because they can't express their natural aggressive feelings. Initially, this is usually caused by not being able to express anger and aggression towards their parents. If one cannot express aggressive feelings or give vent to one's anger life can become a long hard struggle.

Many people suffer from migraine, which, like most headaches, is caused by mental tension. Sufferers from migraine are usually very hostile, not being able to express their resentment, which, although originating with the parents, is often transferred to the therapist if they come for treatment. One patient who came to see me was a 38-year-old woman, married, with three children. She had a lover who she was terrified might reject her. She could only get an orgasm with her husband if she was on top. She never had an orgasm with her lover. She didn't like men. On her first visit after the consultation she told me:

'I got a migraine after seeing you on Thursday. I haven't had one for three years. I couldn't sleep all night.'

At the following session she told me a dream:

'There was a tiny man, a dwarf. I had to be careful not to tread on him. I remembered later that he was bald and had a beard.'

Although not a dwarf, I'm bald and I have a beard.

Biting one's nails or having eczema are other examples of physical symptoms caused by repressed aggressive feelings. Many people have no idea that underneath their placid exterior there lurks an aggressive monster. Some of my patients are quite surprised sometimes when they realise how much anger and resentment they are harbouring. Some find it very difficult to come to terms with it while others are able to express it quite spontaneously. One male patient of mine replied to a follow-up letter I wrote him, saying: 'I have a very bad temper – amazing what you find when you let go, isn't it!'

A common outlet for frustrated aggressive feelings is in so-called 'accidents'. Motor car accidents are very common. Yet few can be called real accidents. In the United States a survey was conducted to establish how many car accidents were caused by faulty cars. It was discovered that only 0.2% of accidents were the fault of mechanical failure. (Reported on Radio 4 'You and Yours', 11 August 1976). Most car accidents are caused by psychological problems resulting in damage to vehicles and people.

Repressed aggression may come out in other ways. Fear of flying is fairly common. Yet figures show that it is safer to fly than to drive a car. Among my patients I find that dreams of plane crashes often occur. Planes can also be phallic symbols. If aggressive feelings are tightly repressed, they can lead to self-destruction. One hears of people who are accident-prone. They are usually acting out their aggressive feelings on themselves or on someone else, or both. Aggression 'is wrong' (some parents instil in their children) so some people feel guilty about their aggressive instincts. Guilt leads to punishment.

Some people compensate for their aggressive feelings by feeling guilty. They become apologetic figures. I once attended a course in psychotherapy at a psychotherapy place in Hampstead. One evening a lecture was given by a woman who had some position in the social services. The talk was terrible. It was boring, ill-prepared and badly delivered. It was a good example of how not to make a speech. The audience was getting restless and fidgety. I could feel the hostility building up. Eventually the agony was over and after some indifferent questions the meeting finished. As the speaker was leaving, everybody began to clap, something that had not happened at any other talk. At first I was taken by surprise that they were clapping this woman who had made such an awful speech. Only afterwards I realised that by clapping the audience were compensating for their hostile feelings.

Some people harbour murderous wishes which they are not aware of. These feelings aren't likely to come out except in psychopathic cases. If these feelings are very strong and the person cannot cope, he may eventually commit suicide.

Others are able to sublimate their aggressive feelings in their work, for instance. Some become surgeons and cut people up. I heard of a heart surgeon who committed suicide at about the age of sixty. He stabbed himself through the heart. Evidently he hadn't come to terms with his murderous wishes in spite of being a heart surgeon.

Aggression has become, quite wrongly, a dirty word. If there wasn't so much repressed aggression, there would be far less violence and crime. Modern life-styles don't always permit one to express aggression. Some jobs, for example, are by nature passive.

Men are predominantly aggressive, while women are predominantly passive. This is the basic sexual arrangement. This can go wrong, as mentioned previously, if one's father is passive and one's mother is aggressive, or if there is a parent missing. One's mental make-up can be compared to a computer. A computer is programmed to respond in certain ways to various stimuli. According to what is fed into the machine, certain information will come out. A child is taught to respond to certain situations or people in a particular way. Consequently, 'feeds' in adult life will produce much the same result as the response the child was taught to produce. When analysing sexual attraction, it's important to remember this. An unnatural home situation may result in a passive man being attracted to an aggressive woman and an aggressive woman being attracted to a passive man.

I find that many patients have difficulty in coming to terms with their repressed feelings of hate and anger. Some patients break off treatment rather than face their hostile feelings. If a patient arrives late for his consultation or refuses to comply with the conditions of treatment, it's usually a sign of repressed hostility. Many people are prevented by their severe hostile feelings from starting therapy. Those very hostile patients who do start, and they usually require daily treatment, make difficult patients and can be very tiring for the therapist.

Normally, aggression is channelled into constructive uses, such as jobs, hobbies, games and so on. Also, men can be aggressive when having sex, much to the delight of their women. Many women find that their men are not aggressive enough in love-making.

Sadists are people who have relatively little guilt about their hostility. They enjoy inflicting pain. A masochist on the other hand feels very guilty about his hostile feelings and punishes himself. A masochist is a repressed sadist. One young American patient who came to see me was very hostile. She compensated for these feelings by being masochistic. She once got these two words confused, however, making a Freudian slip. She told me:

'I didn't want to be alone last Christmas. It was always a big occasion at home. Richard and Christine came over from the States at my invitation. I said I'd pay half their fare. They treated me so badly. I must have been sadistic. No. I got the wrong word. I was being masochistic.'

Paranoia
A paranoiac is someone who believes he's being persecuted when he isn't. He may falsely believe that people are laughing at him or that people don't like him, or are talking about him behind his back, or are rejecting him, or are being inconsiderate or harsh.

Paranoia can be caused by repressed aggression. Some paranoid people cannot express their own hostile feelings and instead see them in other people. This is called projection. Ernest Hemingway was paranoid, at least towards the end of his life, before he finally shot himself. He believed that the FBI were investigating his finances.

Paranoia can also be caused by parents who persecute their children. If you are brought up by parents who watch you, waiting for the slightest excuse to criticise and condemn, it's not surprising if you spend the rest of your life feeling hounded.

A child may take ridicule as a rejection. Quite often, ridicule is used as, and seen as, an act of hostility. Ridicule is often used to lampoon public figures.

Wars may be started by paranoid statesmen. Stalin and Hitler were paranoid, each believing other nations were going to attack their own.

I find that repressed homosexual patients are often paranoid. Some men are afraid of being sexually attacked by their fathers. This can be a wish. Most homosexuals are very suspicious when they come for treatment. One man who came to see me was a successful stockbroker with a family. He said that he suffered from a stammer, although I could hardly discern it. He complained that he did not like the peep-hole in the front door at The Psychotherapy Centre and that he did not like the Principal, who at that time had shoulder-length hair. He was a paranoid, repressed homosexual. It turned out that his father was selfish and unemotional, and was potentially violent, which made the patient scared of him. The patient felt rejected by his father, who was unable to demonstrate any love to him.

Jealousy

Jealousy is an emotional feeling which can be very destructive. Some people confuse jealousy with envy. Envy is a rational feeling, jealousy is not. If you are a man you might envy your neighbour's Rolls Royce or his pretty wife. If you are a woman you might envy their expensive house or the wife's good looks. These feelings are quite natural. On the other hand, if you are resentful, with feelings of hate, you would be feeling jealous.

Jealousy feelings usually have their roots in childhood, when the child, as it grows, has to contend with competition for one parent against the other, or against siblings. Parents are usually at fault. Many a father is jealous of his children, who demand love and attention from their mother. From having his wife all to himself, the father then has to share her with an intruder. Babies require constant supervision and are a full-time occupation for the mother. This jealousy by the father may be reflected in the child, who will sense a competitive element in the family. Boys, especially, may feel a need to compete with father for mother.

A mother, too, may become jealous of her children. She may feel that her husband is paying too much attention to his son. Fathers often identify with their sons, projecting their own ambitions onto the offspring. Mothers may feel resentful towards their daughters, seeing them as competition. As a daughter grows up, she can develop into a good-looking young woman, being sexually attractive to men, including her father.

A son's desire to get rid of his father and have his mother to himself is often referred to as the Oedipus Complex, a term coined by Freud. The legend of King Oedipus belongs to classical antiquity, dramatised by Sophocles, which, although well known, is worth repeating:

Oedipus, son of Laius and Jocasta, rulers of Thebes, was, as an infant, left exposed on a mountain by his father to die because earlier an oracle had warned Laius that the child would be his father's murderer. The child was rescued, was adopted by Polybus, King of Corinth, and grew up as a Corinthian prince. Then the oracle warned him that he was destined to murder his father and marry his mother. Believing Polybus to be his real father, he left Corinth to avoid this fate and during his journey met a man who was, unknown to him, his father, and slew him in a quarrel. He came to

Thebes, where he solved the riddle set by the Sphinx, thus ridding the city of this murderous creature. Out of gratitude, the Thebans made him their King, giving him Jocasta's hand in marriage. She bore him two sons and two daughters. A plague broke out. The Thebans were told by the oracle that the plague would only cease when the murderer of Laius had been driven from the land. Gradually it was revealed that Oedipus, unwittingly, was the guilty one. Appalled by what he discovered, and consumed by guilt, Oedipus blinded himself, and was expelled from Thebes.

The Oedipal myth was regarded by Freud as a useful analogy, describing a son's wish to kill his father and marry his mother, with consequent guilt feelings. Similarly, a daughter may wish to get rid of her mother and have her father to herself. This is sometimes called the Electra Complex.

However, there are other possibilities. A daughter may have an Oedipus Complex, wanting to get rid of her father and monopolise her mother. Or a son may want to have his father to himself. Most children go through these stages at some time in their development, unconsciously working through them. If these feelings are not worked through, they may become fixations affecting the offspring for the rest of his life.

Parents, fathers especially, often feel threatened by their children. A father's hostility towards his son is referred to as the Laius Complex, the parent wanting to harm the child. Although the child may have an Oedipus Complex, something must have caused the child to have these feelings. After all, the child is born innocent, and any actions it subsequently takes must be a result of its environment, particularly parental attitudes. In the Oedipal myth, Laius commits the crime of abandoning the innocent child on a mountainside to perish. It's interesting to note that Freud failed to see this. He was intent on putting the onus on the child. Could this have been a reflection of his own problems? Did he feel guilty about blaming parents?

Some fathers, consciously or unconsciously, see their children as rivals. Once a mother has had her first child, she can no longer devote all her attention to her husband. A rival has been born.

Some fathers may see the birth of a child as a reminder of the birth of a sibling in their own childhood. The same could apply to a mother. These feelings of jealousy can cause some couples not to have any children. I have come across men and women who refuse to have children for this reason. One man I once met didn't want any children. His wife allowed herself to become pregnant, hoping to win him round. When he found out that she was pregnant, he left her. Children, especially the first-born, can trigger problems in a family.

One young female patient who was seeing me realised that her father was jealous of his son.

'My father said that my brother had tried to take our step-mother away from him. He saw my brother as a rival.'

However careful a parent might be in preparing a child for the arrival of a sibling, jealousy will inevitably occur. The birth of a new baby in a family can have a traumatic effect on older siblings. These feelings of jealousy can often be very difficult to resolve. A newborn child, especially the first-born, gets a lot of attention, sometimes being pampered and spoilt. When the next child arrives, the first may suddenly find itself being dropped like a hot potato, all the fuss and attention going to the new baby.

Many parents, as well as relatives and friends, are insensitive about this, not realising what effect a newborn child is having on the rest of the family. Many children manage to work through their jealousy feelings. But some don't, going through life with a chip on their shoulder, affecting their work, marriage and relationships. Many people are not aware of their jealousy feelings, although these feelings are bound to surface in one form or another, sooner or later. Unless jealousy is resolved in childhood or therapy, it can have a devastating effect. It's the green-eyed monster which eats away at your insides. Jealousy often makes sexual relationships and marriage impossible. It can make people hate anyone who might be a rival, whether in a sex situation, or in a work situation where a younger person may represent a threat. Quite often, these situations are imaginary, the jealous person fantasising about situations which don't exist.

When dealing with patients, a therapist must be aware of feelings of jealousy that may be felt by the patient. There could be sibling rivalry among patients; one patient may see another patient as his hated brother or sister. This was brought home to me when I took on two sisters as patients. Taking on the second, younger sister, some two years after the first, had a very traumatic effect on the elder patient. This was in spite of the fact that it was she who had encouraged her younger sister to come for therapy.

It is best that patients who are being treated by the same therapist do not come into contact with each other. The therapist should avoid making references to other patients. Most patients, seeing the therapist as a parent, don't want to think that he has any other patients, who could be seen as sibling rivals. Some patients are over-concerned about other patients, being curious and asking questions about them, which should not be answered by the therapist, but analysed.

One patient laughingly told me:

'I have a fantasy that I'm your only patient!'

Many patients don't like waiting in the reception room. They want to come straight into the consulting-room without seeing anybody else.

Very jealous people often believe that their lover or spouse is being unfaithful. No amount of reassurance or proof to the contrary will alter their belief. On two occasions I have been consulted by men who wanted me to hypnotise their lovers to discover whether they were being faithful. I explained that this was their problem, not their lover's, but they didn't embark on treatment.

Jealousy and rivalry can often lead to murderous wishes which, although seldom carried out, can exist in people's fantasies and dreams. Patients often have murderous wishes towards their parents, which can come out in dreams. Many sons see their father as barring their way to their mother. One young male patient told me this dream:

'I was outside the back door of a pub. I wanted to go in. The barman stood in front of me, staring at me. He just stood and stared. So I beat him to death on the floor. I couldn't stop myself. He had a smug look on his face.'

Another young male patient told me this dream:

'Dad came back from the pub. He was legless, nasty and stupid. He was having a go at Mum. Then he came in and had a go at me. I then started strangling him. I had him up against the wall.'

Some female patients have murderous wishes towards their mothers. One female patient told me this:

'I used to have a dream as a child, always the same one. I dreamt that my mother's head was in a butcher's window.'

Another patient, a middle-aged female, told me this dream:

'I killed a woman.'

Other female patients have murderous feelings towards their fathers. Another female patient told me these two dreams:

'President Carter dropped dead while jogging. I was distressed.'

'A man's body was pulled out of a pool. He'd stabbed himself. I looked – he had a knife stuck into his erect penis.'

Sibling hatred and murderous feelings can also reveal themselves in dreams. A young female patient had very hostile feelings towards her brother. She told me this dream:

'I was in a pub with my brother. He got angry. He picked up a chair and hit me. I thought he was going to kill me. He hit me in the ribs. I eventually killed him. I stabbed him twice.'

Some patients are quite conscious of their murderous feelings. One young patient, who hated her father, told me:

'I remember I once wanted to kill my father – so did my mother. I put some Ajax in his tea, but he never drank it.'

SIX

Parental attitudes

Parents often don't realise how their attitudes affect their children. Sometimes parental attitudes are quite illogical. One patient told me:

'When I was studying for my 'O' levels, mother didn't give me enough time. She considered social activities more important. Yet at the same time she said: "You won't fail your 'O' levels, will you?"'

This same patient, who came from a respectable middle-class family, also told me:

'Mother used to be very nice and polite to people, and then bitch about them afterwards behind their backs. I wondered if she did the same to me.'

Parents often give presents to their children without giving sufficient thought as to what the child would like. One patient, in hypnosis, told me:

'Once, on my birthday, Mum and Dad gave me a present. I was in bed. I opened it. It was a stamp album. I was *so* disappointed. I'm not interested in stamps. It's not a normal birthday present; I would have preferred money. I felt ungrateful; I wasn't appreciating the present. Bloody stamps. Boring, giving me this black book. Trying to do something to me. *His* idea.'

Not only did the patient feel angry and disappointed, but he also felt guilty at being ungrateful and not appreciating the present.

Some parents, especially mothers, are socially ambitious for their children. One male patient, who was 31 years old and had never been married, told me:

'My mother used to say to me: "You must marry above your class." Because of this I never dared bring a girlfriend home to meet my parents.'

Other parents may have preconceived ideas as to what their children will or will not be able to do. One patient, a divorcee, told me:

'When I was young my father told me that I wouldn't ever dance or pass my driving test.'

Both these actions were probably sexually symbolic, showing the father's anxiety about his daughter's sexual feelings.

Others, not just parents, can make children feel very guilty. One young female patient, who used to be a ballet dancer, told me:

'I've always felt guilty about giving up dancing. A friend of my parents once said: "How dare she give up dancing after all her parents spent on her!"'

In reality the truth was somewhat different. The patient went on:

'My parents didn't understand me; didn't understand what I was doing. They pretended to like ballet, coming to watch me dance. When I said I was giving it up, my mother said she was quite pleased, as she didn't really like ballet.'

Another patient told me:

'My parents believe that children have a duty to their parents. That they should be grateful for being born.'

Some parents want to keep up appearances, being concerned at what other people think. An Irish patient told me:

'I'm concerned at what other people think. In Dublin my mother and father used to worry about what the neighbours would say.'

Sometimes parents are insensitive towards their children. Some parents have sex in front of their young children, not realising how much a young child or baby can be aware of. If a child doesn't understand what's going on, he can be frightened. Patients often recollect early experiences. One patient remembered, in hypnosis, being in a cot in her parents' bedroom:

'My parents are fucking in the bed next to me. Horrible grunting noises.'

A young child can be aware of what's going on even if he doesn't understand.

Often parents don't encourage their children to grow up and be independent. They want (even though it may be unconscious) to keep their children at home for their own pleasure. One young patient, in her late twenties, told me:

'I'm forcing myself to go out in the evenings. When I was living at home I never went out for two years. I came home from work, had dinner, watched television and went to bed. I did that for two years!'

Some parents use their children as pawns in their squabbles. One patient told me:

'When my parents used to argue, they'd try to get me to take sides. Then they'd make up and be against me.'

Other parents show phoney concern. They believe that they are acting in the interest of their children, when in fact they have selfish motives. One patient told me:

'My parents moulded us into what they wanted: perfect children. A perfect child doesn't cry; doesn't get angry.'

Sometimes parents confuse their children with contradictory statements. One middle-aged patient, who came from a very respectable family, told me, in hypnosis:

'I worry about my ability to do things. My parents always said I didn't do well enough; that I must do better. Mother also said that granny had said: "To praise is wrong."'

It wasn't surprising that this patient felt insecure about his abilities. Many parents are quick to chide, but slow to praise.

SEVEN

Choosing a sex partner and getting married
As a species, human beings are basically monogamous: one man, one woman. There are and there have been exceptions, however. In some societies men may take on more than one wife, while in others it has been known for women to take on more than one husband, although in most countries bigamy is illegal. Having more than one spouse was probably introduced in some societies where there was an imbalance of sexes and procreation was important. Nowadays, in most countries, the sexes are more or less evenly balanced, with only occasional imbalances as during a world war, when there is a reduction in the male population.

Monogamy leads to the marriage arrangement. In every corner of the world, even amongst the most primitive tribes, there exists some form of marriage. There is a strong natural urge in all humans for pair-bonding. This is the basic structure for a family, the children needing both a father and a mother. In modern Western societies marriage has lost much of its sanctity, becoming more of a conventional arrangement. Many people, with some justification, argue that there is no need to marry unless you intend to have children or there is a tax advantage. Even with this more liberal outlook, the pair-bonding urge still holds.

Most of us believe that one aim in life is to marry and procreate. This probably applies more to women than men, as most women have strong maternal instincts.

There are various reasons why people marry. Some people feel the need to belong, replacing a parent with husband or wife. This is the natural process of growing up; leaving the family nest and starting a family of your own.

Marriage is also a form of security, conforming to an established process. Some people feel that they might be considered peculiar if they don't marry. If all your friends and acquaintances are married, you might find yourself ostracised, not fitting into an established pattern. You might also be seen as a threat to people who are married; a lone wolf in search of a partner. They may think you might steal their spouse.

Some people are afraid of being considered homosexual if they are not married. Many repressed (and overt) homosexuals marry, overcompensating for their feelings. Some homosexuals may spend all their lives trying to prove that they're straight. Many men and women who have repressed homosexual tendencies are heterosexually promiscuous to prove to themselves or to others that all is well. Many repressed homosexuals never manage to marry, although they may lead a very active, normal sex-life. In discussing sexual relationships and marriage, it's important to consider the effects of repressed homosexuality, which can explain some people's bizarre sexual behaviour.

Although there are other reasons why some people never marry, parental influence is the greatest single cause. Consciously or unconsciously, many parents, particularly mothers, don't want their children to leave home and marry. Many children remain faithful to their parents, rather than finding a suitable partner of the opposite sex. Some people don't marry until their parents are dead, the death giving them a sense of release and freedom. They no longer feel guilty about getting married, once their parents are no longer around.

Judging by the divorce rate, which in Britain is increasing year by year, many people either marry for the wrong reason or make a neurotic choice. In Britain, about one marriage in three ends in divorce. Choosing a suitable sex partner is not easy. You are greatly influenced by your upbringing. If you have fairly well-balanced parents, you are likely to choose a fairly well-balanced partner. On the other hand, if your parents are neurotic, you will probably make a neurotic choice of partner, or not marry at all. By marrying, you are, unconsciously, replacing a parent with a spouse. If you aren't emotionally independent of your parents you will find it difficult to marry, let alone have a happy marriage.

Often one can spot a family trait in marriages, children following their parents' examples. Sons of aggressive mothers tend to marry aggressive women, while daughters of passive fathers tend to marry passive men. These traits may continue from generation to generation.

Why do people have children?
Both men and women, especially women, have a natural desire to have children. This desire can sometimes become strong enough for a woman to produce a phantom pregnancy. (It also has been known for a man to have a phantom pregnancy.) There is the obvious reason of wanting to procreate, to keep the family going, to keep the species going. Many people feel that their life is unfulfilled unless they produce

offspring.

There are also other reasons why people have children, reasons which may not always be consciously apparent. Some reasons may be neurotic, some not. Children can be company, they can be playthings. They can be objects of love or from whom love can be demanded.

Some people's reasons for having children are selfish, although they may not be aware of it. Some fathers want sons to identify with, reliving their own (probably inadequate) lives through their sons. Or fathers may want daughters to drool over, giving some expression to their repressed incestuous wishes. If often happens that when the daughter reaches her teens, starting to have boyfriends, the father becomes jealous and angry. Some fathers refuse to allow their daughters to wear make-up: it may remind the father of his incestuous wishes, or he may not want his daughter to be attractive to other men. Or he may lose interest in her once she begins to develop secondary sexual characteristics, not wanting to become aware of his feelings towards her.

One female patient told me that her father completely lost interest in her when she reached the age of puberty. From being a fond, interested parent, he became aloof and distant. This had a traumatic effect on the patient at a time when she particularly needed her father. He could not face his own sexual feelings towards his daughter, which resulted in him withdrawing his love completely. Many fathers, if they were truthful, would like to have sexual intercourse with their daughters.

As I have already mentioned, some parents have children in order that the children will look after the parents in their old age.

Other people have children to prove that they're sexually adequate. In some countries a large family can be a source of pride as well as evidence of sexual prowess. For a man to discover that he's infertile can be a traumatic experience, rather like finding out that he's castrated.

Some married couples have children because it's the accepted way of life; like getting married, it's an established custom. Other married couples are fearful of what people may think if there are no children in the marriage. Could there be something wrong? What will the neighbours say? Or couples may have children to please their own parents, for the latter to have grandchildren.

Unfortunately, you cannot choose your parents; you're stuck with what you have: good, bad or indifferent. Too many people have children for the wrong reasons. Having children is a responsible decision, not an event that should be entered into lightly.

EIGHT

The conscious and the unconscious
As we grow up, the conscious mind and the unconscious mind normally come to a workable arrangement. Unconscious feelings and desires are expressed in such a way that they are acceptable to the conscious mind. This may produce positive results or negative results. The more balanced the conscious and unconscious are the more positive the person will be, while the less balanced they are the more negative and destructive the person will be.

Many of the natural unconscious feelings a child has may be repressed by the parents. These are feelings which are not acceptable to the parents. This repression may cause problems later in life. This balance, or sometimes imbalance, between the conscious and the unconscious mind is achieved over a considerable period of time, from birth until we are into our late teens. As well as parental influence, the environment and religion can leave their mark on a child.

There is always a barrier between the unconscious and the conscious mind. This barrier is sometimes referred to as the censor or 'parent voice' inside us. This 'voice' dictates much of what is acceptable and what isn't. Because of the length of time a human being takes to develop his mental faculties, any problems that are caused by parents may take a long time to sort out in psychotherapy.

As well as the major divisions, conscious and

unconscious, in the mind, there is also the subconscious, which is a kind of 'store-room' for memories. This part of the mind is particularly active during times of learning.

The unconscious mind, being stronger than the conscious mind, dictates most of our behaviour. The conscious mind has a certain amount of choice, but only within the confines of the unconscious. Because the unconscious is stronger and not directly accessible, changes in behaviour are not always easy to bring about. There is no direct communication with the unconscious.

This mental set-up may lead to a situation where we follow an unconscious desire or need without realising it. We may do things without knowing why. This in itself is not necessarily a problem, but problems will arise when there are conflicts between unconscious desires and conscious behaviour. Many patients, once they begin to recover, find that their interests change, their likes and dislikes change; they may even find that they are in the wrong job. Psychotherapy often has a dramatic effect on a patient's life.

In addition to controlling the natural functions of the body, such as breathing, heartbeat and digestion, the unconscious is also concerned with feelings and emotions, and it's in this area that we find problems. The natural instincts in some of us may, for one reason or another, have been thwarted from expressing themselves positively. Most of us at times say or do things for which we find it difficult to give a logical explanation. Yet there is always an unconscious reason to be found.

The conscious mind, the part that we are aware of, is mostly the logical or thinking brain. We may be aware of what we are doing and we may think that it's quite natural without necessarily knowing why. We may make a joke, for instance, and laugh, without knowing why it's funny. Only by analysing the joke can we find the basis for our pleasure. A parapraxis (a Freudian slip) is a good example of the unconscious mind breaking through our conscious guard. One man I knew was concerned about being overweight. He intended to say that he wanted to get fit but instead he said 'I want to get fat.' Noel Coward, interviewed on television, said 'lavatory' instead of 'library'. Freudian slips can sometimes be amusing as well as revealing. A male patient, in his twenties, once said to me during a session:

'There's so little of my childhood I can't remember. No, I mean so much of my childhood.'

A female patient once told me:

'Last night my boyfriend said: "I want to kill you" when he meant to say: "I want to kiss you." He was very embarrassed.'

These slips can also occur in writing. Whether it's a slip of the tongue or the pen, the message comes through. One patient once made a slip of the pen. After she went into hypnosis she signalled that she couldn't speak, which sometimes happens when patients have a strong resistance to therapy. I handed her a block of paper and a pencil, asking her to write whatever was on her mind. She wrote very slowly. When she came out of hypnosis I asked her what she'd written. She said: 'I can't say anything.' I then took the pad and saw that in fact she'd written: 'I can say anything.' I had difficulty in convincing her that she had really written this.

How much does the unconscious influence our lives? Important decisions, such as choice of job or choice of marriage partner, are largely influenced by the unconscious. Many people are in the wrong job, having made a neurotic choice. Some patients, after analysis, change jobs, usually choosing something quite different. The same applies to marriage. Some patients discover, much to their disconcertion, that they have married the wrong person. Some patients may break off treatment rather than accept this. Similarly, in other ways, some major, some minor, we are influenced by something over which we have no direct control.

Most accidents are probably caused by unconscious desires. Quite often, accidents, including the already mentioned car accidents, are an outlet for repressed aggressive feelings; feelings which should be directed towards someone or something else. Some accidents are caused by guilt feelings resulting in an unconscious desire for self-punishment.

Dreams
People have long been intrigued by the meaning of dreams. Everybody dreams during sleep, dreams occurring several times a night. We may not always remember our dreams, a fact which encourages some people to believe that they don't dream. Some people remember much of what they dream, while others remember little or nothing. The ability to remember dreams is not usually important except in psychotherapy, where associations with dreams can be useful, allowing the patient to discover what is going on in his unconscious.

Some people believe that dreams are prophetic, an indication as to what will happen. In the Old Testament, Joseph got out of prison by interpreting

Pharaoh's dreams, but there is no evidence that dreams foretell the future except insofar as dreams are largely wishes and consequently reflect what the dreamer (consciously and/or unconsciously) wants to happen. This being the case, he is likely to take actions which are in keeping with the dream. Often these actions are brought about unconsciously.

There is also the coincidence factor. There may be a serious plane crash, for instance, which many people report having dreamt of the night before. But every night thousands of people dream of plane crashes. One young patient of mine lost both her parents in the bad air disaster outside Paris. She said that she had dreamt about the crash the night before, claiming that it was a prophetic dream. As her analysis progressed, it appeared that the dream exposed her deep hostile feelings towards her parents, wishing that they would be killed.

Dreaming is essential for our well-being. Researchers have told us that sleepers who were wakened on entering paradoxical sleep (the time when we dream) but allowed to sleep during orthodox sleep, had shown disturbing results. It has been claimed that prolonged dream-deprivation could provoke a psychotic state. Dreams occur mainly during the latter part of sleep.

Dreams are a language of the unconscious, which is very useful in telling us what is going on in our inner mind. Dreams are also an emotional release for the unconscious mind. Freud referred to dreams as 'The royal road to the unconscious'. Dream scrutiny is an important part of therapy, not only enabling the patient to understand himself better, gaining insight, but helping the analyst to see what is going on in the patient's mind. If the patient is unconsciously contemplating breaking off therapy, quite often a dream will indicate that this may happen, enabling the therapist to sort it out with the patient.

Much of what we dream, being repressed material, is not allowed to surface into the conscious. Many painful or unpleasant feelings are kept locked away. Some patients find difficulty in accepting their strong aggressive or sexual feelings. Sometimes these feelings do surface unexpectedly, which may give the patient a shock. In analysis, these repressed feelings are normally allowed to surface slowly, in small doses, enabling the patient to accept them.

Dreams are usually symbolic, which explains some of the weird dreams that we produce. Dreams can also be a clever construction, rather like a symbolic painting. After examining one of her dreams, one of my patients found it difficult to believe that she could have produced such a work of art. Dreams can be complex and a therapist has to be careful not to impose interpretations. Dreams are produced by the dreamer, who has his own dream language, and it's important to remember that it's his associations that matter.

Sometimes dreams can be simple and direct, expressing a conscious as well as an unconscious wish.

NINE

Symptoms, causes and treatment
When dealing with emotional problems, many people confuse symptoms with causes and precipitating factors. Symptoms are indicators. They tell us when something isn't functioning properly, as does an indicator on the instrument panel of a motor-car. In the treatment of physical problems, pain is an important symptom. In addition to telling us that something is wrong, pain has the dual purpose of pinpointing the problem and stopping us using that particular part of the body, to prevent further damage. A physician can use the pain to enable him to diagnose the cause and administer suitable treatment. Normally, he should not treat the symptom. He could give you a 'pain-killer' and send you away. This would be treating the symptom, not the cause. If you have a broken leg he must recognise this and see that your leg is properly set, not merely ease the pain.

With emotional problems the same principle applies; causes should be treated, not symptoms. Unfortunately, many physicians and some therapists, especially therapists who have been medically trained, don't apply this basic criterion to the emotional problems they have to deal with. Too often, physicians administer unsuitable treatment for problems which originate in the mind. Aspirins, for instance, are usually prescribed for headaches. Yet headaches are nearly always caused by an emotional disturbance. Aspirins can be harmful; they occasionally cause bleeding in the stomach which can lead to ulcers, even death.

Generally speaking, the body can look after itself. Better food, better living conditions and a healthier environment have helped to eradicate most diseases. Apart from physical damage, there is not a lot that should go wrong with your body, provided you keep fit.

Most people who visit their GP are suffering from complaints which, directly or indirectly, are caused in the mind. GP's are not trained to deal with emotional problems or with psychogenic problems (physical symptoms with emotional causes). They usually write out a prescription, often for a psychotropic drug which at best may help temporarily to alleviate a nervous condition or a psychosomatic symptom. Valium and Librium are two well-known drugs which are prescribed for anxiety and depression. Sleeping pills are also prescribed in large quantities. Prescribing these drugs is symptom-suppression, not treatment of causes.

Psychotropic drugs are unnatural and can be harmful. The body inevitably becomes immune to the drug, so that larger doses are needed or a new drug has to be found, a fact that large drug companies are not slow to exploit. Drugs can lead to dependency and addiction. Some can also lead to death, either intentionally or not. Many people take sleeping pills when they can't sleep. If one is not enough, they take another. By the time they have taken three or four, they are drowsy, they still can't sleep and don't know what they are doing. In this situation, it's only too easy to take an overdose.

It's important to know which problems are of physical origin and which are of emotional origin, and to consult the appropriate practitioner in each case.

Some physicians often throw up a smoke-screen by saying that one needs to be medically qualified to practise as a psychotherapist in case a patient is suffering from a physical complaint, not a psychological one. In my experience I have never come across a patient seeking psychotherapy for a problem with physical origins. Usually it's the other way round. Many patients with emotional problems are fed up with being fobbed off with pills and useless advice from the medical profession.

Sometimes physicians don't correctly diagnose problems which require physical treatment. Some years ago there was a case reported when a patient consulted her GP, a woman, complaining of severe headaches. The GP simply gave her 'pain-killers' and sent her away. It was some weeks later that the patient decided to go into hospital for a check-up. It was discovered that she had a brain tumour.

Many therapists who are medically trained have misguided ideas as to the causes of emotional problems. In treating physical problems the links between causes and symptoms usually follow a definite pattern and are constant. The rule normally applies to all patients: same symptom, same cause.

When dealing with emotional problems this is not the case. The link between symptoms and causes may vary from patient to patient; there is no clear-cut link between symptoms and causes. What applies to one patient may not apply to another, although, once the cause and symptom have established a relationship, they usually remain constant within the particular individual.

In psychotherapy, each patient should be treated individually, with an open mind as to what the cause

99

could be. In addition, it's important to allow the patient to discover for himself what the origins of his problem are. Telling a patient what the cause of his problem is, even if accurate, isn't going to solve the problem and may increase resistance in the patient. Interpretation is one of the most common faults amongst psychotherapists and psycho-analysts, especially if they are medically trained. Medical practitioners tend to be dogmatic as well as authoritarian, telling their patients what is wrong with them. If an analyst behaves in this manner, it may be reflecting a sense of insecurity in the analyst, who may feel that he must demonstrate that he's in charge of treatment.

Many people, especially physicians, are confused when confronted with problems which are psychogenic. This can result in physicians treating a psychogenic problem medically, therefore incorrectly. As a result many people follow their example and look for symptom-suppression rather than cause-cure. Asthma, hay-fever and skin disorders can be psychogenic problems and, if so, should be treated psychologically, not medically.

Some patients, at the consultation, ask me questions like: 'Have you treated people with the same problem as mine?' or: 'What success have you had with my kind of problem?' These questions are irrelevant: one can only treat each case individually. In emotional problems, the symptom may tell us something is wrong, but not usually what is wrong, nor why. Different people with the same symptom may have different causes for their symptom.

Certain symptoms may give a general indication as to what may be the cause. A person who bites his nails, for instance, is probably expressing repressed aggression. However, one would still have to discover what's causing the aggression, as well as why it's being repressed.

With emotional problems, as well as there being symptoms and causes, there are precipitating factors. A precipitating factor can trigger off a symptom without being its cause. This can create further confusion in the minds of some people who believe that the precipitating factor is the cause of the problem. Hay-fever is a good example. Pollen can precipitate hay-fever but the cause is likely to be an emotional one. Pollen can irritate the nasal tissues, causing great discomfort, affecting some people but not others. You could avoid hay-fever by avoiding pollen, if this was possible, but this would not be a cure. Taking an antihistamine may relieve hay-fever, but this would be treating the symptom.

Something irritating the mind can manifest itself in a physical irritation. In such a case the emotional problem should be treated, not the physical symptom. Skin problems are often caused, or precipitated by, emotional problems. Many people with psoriasis, eczema or herpes have found that their skin disorder has disappeared or diminished during psychotherapy, though, of course, the symptom is not itself treated, and these benefits are usually incidental ones when the patient has sought help for an apparently unconnected problem. Most physicians attempt to treat skin problems with ointments and creams, with little success.

As I have already mentioned, a good therapist treats the patient's whole personality, working on a broad front, not making narrow excursions into the unconscious. As shown elsewhere in this book, some patients have stopped smoking or biting their nails without my knowing that they were affected by that particular symptom.

A patient who recovered from a particular symptom without telling me that it was one of her problems was a 26-year-old girl. She came to see me as she found that she had lost her zest and drive for life, as well as suffering from depression. She lived with her boyfriend, but seldom had sex, as she didn't enjoy it, not getting orgasms. She told me that she'd had two abortions. Her father had been in the Royal Air Force which had necessitated the family travelling abroad a lot. The patient didn't get on with her father, especially after he started drinking heavily when she was about 13 years old. She also told me at the consultation that she got on well with her mother, although later in her therapy she realised that this was a false assumption. The patient had been to see two hypnotists; she said neither had helped her. The first she found brusque and cold. The second was a woman who used hypnosis which appeared to help but, when the patient ended her therapy the depression returned, its causes not having been tackled.

I noticed at the consultation that the patient had a shiny face as if a cream had been applied. This was consistent every time she came to see me, which was twice a week. After about three months of treatment I noticed that she no longer had this shiny look on her face. When I enquired about it, she told me that she had suffered from spots on her face, putting an ointment on every day. She had been doing this since she was 15 years old, but it hadn't improved her condition. Her face had cleared up after three months in therapy and more than a year later her face was still free of blemishes. This patient had never mentioned her skin condition until I asked her about it. She was under the impression that it had a physical cause.

Another case was that of a young man in his twenties who came to see me for various problems including homosexual tendencies. He was very hostile towards people generally, a hostility which stemmed from deep resentment towards his parents, particularly his father. At the end of his second summer in therapy he told me that he'd only just realised that he hadn't suffered from hay-fever that year. He'd never told me that hay-fever was one of his problems, as he didn't think that it was a psychological problem. Treating his whole personality had resolved his hay-fever.

I have found it quite common for patients who bite their nails to stop without realising that the symptom was part of their problem. Some of my female patients have been delighted to find themselves sporting long fingernails. Quite often this has happened without the patient discussing the nail-biting with me.

One 47-year-old female patient who had come to see me to sort out her inability to form a lasting relationship with a man told me one day:

'For the first time in my life I have long nails. I've stopped biting and picking them.'

Another patient, a man in his twenties who was having treatment for a sexual problem, told me out of the blue one day that he hadn't bitten his nails for two weeks.

In both these cases I was unaware that the patient was a nail-biter. One doesn't always have to know the symptom to effect a recovery. In proper psychotherapy, the whole personality is treated, not separate symptoms.

Some patients come for treatment with a single

symptom, say depression. After a time the depression disappears, but the patient may continue with treatment, realising that he is benefitting in other ways. He may discover that he has potential which he never knew of. On the other hand, some patients who seek therapy for a particular problem, say overweight, may find that they improve in other ways but remain overweight. It may be the last symptom to go.

As most emotional problems are caused by a bad relationship between parents and children, and as this relationship usually covers many years, therapy may take a long time to sort problems out. This applies to most patients seeking therapy.

Some symptoms are subtle in their behaviour. Migraine, for instance, can be brought on by physical factors, such as eating cheese or chocolate. Or it can have no obvious precipitating factor at all. Headaches and migraines are usually caused by tension in the mind. Often this tension is caused by unresolved problems concerning one's parents.

One young female patient of 16 who came to see me for various problems told me that she used to get headaches until she had a row with her mother and walked out to go to live with her father. Her parents had got divorced when she was 12 years old.

Emotional problems can cause physical symptoms both directly and indirectly. A cold, for instance, is caused by a virus which will only affect the body when conditions are appropriate. Some people seem never to get a cold, while others get one cold after another. The mind can produce the physical conditions which are suitable for the cold virus. A sick mind can produce a sick body, while a healthy mind can produce a healthy body.

This link between causes and symptoms is of special relevance in treating emotional problems. The symptom is often a safety valve whereby the patient is able to express his problem in an acceptable form (acceptable, that is, to himself). Someone suffering from dermatitis may be suffering from an emotional irritation; overweight people may be protecting themselves; a person with a paralysed arm may want to strangle someone. These are strong links and serve a valid purpose for the person concerned. This is one reason why it can be dangerous for an unqualified person to meddle with hypnosis, attempting to remove symptoms by using suggestion treatment. Some people believe that a medical qualification is sufficient or desirable for a practitioner to use hypnosis. This belief is due to ignorance and indoctrination.

Removing a symptom by suggestion treatment may, like symptom-suppression by drugs, have only temporary results or cause the patient to develop other symptoms.

Because in many cases symptoms have been with the patient for many years, they can become a form of security. Something the patient is familiar with and feels at home with. Quite often people are well aware of a neurotic symptom yet quite incapable of controlling it. The longer a patient has suffered from a problem, the longer, usually, it takes to resolve it.

Sometimes, psychological problems lie dormant, only surfacing at times when a stressful stimulus affects the individual. Some people go right through life without realising that they have a hidden emotional disorder. When problems do arise, they may do so at any time in one's life, but usually symptoms caused by emotional disorders appear early in life. Some people manage to rationalise or fool themselves that everything is all right when it isn't. Then some traumatic experience throws up symptoms which show that something is wrong. Leaving home for the first time, getting married, having children, losing a job, death of a relative, retirement, can all produce neurotic symptoms. Again, one must remember that these are precipating factors, not the underlying causes of the problem. Sometimes, symptoms may appear and then disappear without any apparent reason. The mind is very complex, and whatever symptoms appear, the way to resolve the problem is to have adequate psychotherapy, dealing with fundamental causes.

A common misconception is that people's psychological difficulties go back to a single incident in childhood. Some therapists, who should know better, also believe this. One female patient told me that she had been to see a psychiatrist. When she told him that she had been sexually molested as a child, he got very excited, believing that he'd discovered the cause of her problem. She was intelligent enough to realise that he wasn't a competent therapist and didn't go back to see him.

This misconception, that psychological problems originate in a single incident in childhood, may be due to the many fictional dramatisations in books, plays and films, where all is solved once the discovery is made relating the problem to a traumatic event in childhood. This may make a good story, fitting neatly into the plot, but unfortunately it's seldom true. If it were, it would make the work of therapists much easier, and treatment for the patient much pleasanter and quicker.

However, occasionally one comes across a case where the problem goes back to a particular incident in childhood. Such a case was a woman who came to consult me because she was afraid of cats. This did not normally cause her any undue concern, but she and her husband were going abroad for a holiday where, she had been told, there were a lot of cats, especially in restaurants. She was a 45-year-old housewife who was happily married with two grown-up children with whom she got on well.

She told me that her phobia went back as far as she could remember. Other animals didn't bother her; she owned a dog but couldn't be in the same room as a cat. She didn't fear that cats would attack her, but she was frightened they might touch her. If a cat came into the room, she had to stand on a chair or walk out. She said she felt stupid about her problem.

She didn't appear to have any other neurotic symptoms, her emotional background being quite healthy. She'd had a good relationship with her father, who had recently died. She also go on well with her mother, although she said her childhood had been lonely. She had a brother, but he was five years older. As she was due to go away in two weeks' time, I said I would try to help her using hypnosis, but added I couldn't guarantee any results. I don't normally take on short-term patients, except in certain cases, and I felt this was one of them.

On her first visit after the consultation, she told me that, as a baby, she used to scream in her pram if a cat came near. This she had been told; she couldn't remember it. I tried hypnosis, to which she had a moderate response. She opened her eyes once and then closed them. After some time she got in her mind a picture of a cat's head.

'It's large and fills everything. It's fluffy and soft and

is licking my face, but it's not an unpleasant feeling.'

She then opened her eyes and was out of hypnosis. She was amazed. She had thought that she was in a pram and the cat's head had filled the opening made by the pram's hood. The cat had wriggled round, then jumped off, but it wasn't frightening.

On her next visit, in hypnosis, she saw a dark tunnel.

'There's a railway line with a grass slope. I'm going into this dark tunnel. I see two yellow eyes getting bigger and bigger. I don't like this very much. There's a roar in the tunnel . . . I'm out now in the sunshine and can see the grass.'

Again she opened her eyes before I had taken her out of hypnosis. She said that she was afraid of going into the tunnel again.

'It wasn't the same cat as last time. I recognise the piece of railway. There was no train, just a rushing noise. I felt that cats have no bodies, only faces. I used to live near Croydon as a child and I can remember Croydon station. It wasn't built up in those days; there were open fields. The tunnel allowed road traffic to pass under the railway. I was alone in the tunnel. It's all very disturbing.'

She had a better response to hypnosis on her third visit when she could remember sitting upright in a pram.

'A cat is walking round the pram, rubbing itself against the wheels, meowing all the time. Another cat is on my feet. It's smaller, and black. Again I'm alone in the dark. The cat's got its feet on mine and its face in mine. It has yellow eyes. It doesn't do anything and gets down from the pram. I'm frightened.'

Out of hypnosis, she told me that a maid used to take her for walks in the pram, leaving her to go to meet a boyfriend.

On the fourth visit she told me that her attitude to 'these creatures' was changing. In hypnosis, she thought there was a cat in the room.

'It's rubbing itself against my legs. Now it's up on my chair. It's like a small dog. I'm not frightened. Now it's gone away. I have a picture of a cat stalking and catching a bird. It's black and white. I should try to touch cats. I don't know what they feel like.' That was her last visit before she went off on holiday.

As she was a short-term patient, I used hypnosis on all her four visits after the consultation. This isn't what I normally do, as many new patients imagine that whether they will progress or not depends entirely on whether they go easily into hypnosis. If hypnosis were tried on that false basis, many of these people would break off treatment prematurely. In some cases I need to defer hypnosis for a considerable time.

This patient received mental images which she described in hypnosis. I said little, other than to suggest, when she was in hypnosis, that she would remember the causes of her problem.

Some months later I wrote to her, enquiring as to how she was getting on. She replied, saying:

'I was intending writing to you because there has been a tremendous improvement over my "cat problem". I am relaxed and if a cat comes into the room I take no notice whatever. With a bit of help from my husband I need to handle a cat once or twice and then, I feel sure, all will be well. There is certainly no question of standing on chairs or leaving restaurants any more – thank goodness!'

As I believe that long-term follow-ups are important, I wrote to her again eight years later, and she replied as follows:

'I was pleased to receive your letter as I had intended writing to you many times. My progress has gone from strength to strength and you can chalk up a successful cure.

'About four years ago my daughter-in-law's cat had eight kittens. I was very involved in this situation with "mother" cat and kittens to the extent that we kept one kitten for ourselves. She is a pretty black cat now and a great joy to the whole household. Could you ask for more proof of my progress?'

This patient was lucky; her problem centred on her experiences with cats while she was still a baby. This kind of traumatic incident can have a frightening effect on a child, usually frightening enough for the memory to be repressed, as in this case. For this type of problem, hypnosis is invaluable.

I find that many patients repress unpleasant childhood experiences, but these problems are usually accompanied by others, such as a bad relationship with parents, which take much longer to sort out.

Some therapists look for a specific experience from childhood which has been forgotten or repressed. This is no more than gimmick therapy. It's presuming the cause without knowing. Proper therapy is an investigation, an exploration into the mind. One doesn't always know what to expect, although a good therapist may have some idea as to the main cause of his patient's problem.

Some patients are obsessional about their symptoms. The symptom can seem all-important. I have encountered patients who arranged a consultation to discuss their problem, but had no intention of resolving it. The symptom had become a prized possession, like a soldier's war wound, which he is proud of, wanting to tell people how he got it. This kind of patient, because of the nature of his problem, cannot be helped. His mental make-up is such that he is only concerned about his symptom, wishing to be assured that no-one can help him. He's a type of hypochondriac; he's only interested in his symptoms, with no real desire to recover.

Soon after I started in practice, I was consulted by a 58-year-old man who said he wanted me to use hypnosis for his speech impediment. During the consultation, I noticed that he spoke with no apparent difficulty. He told me that he'd had his problem since he was a child, adding that he'd consulted four or five hypnotists over a period of about 25 years. He'd also tried acupuncture, but all to no avail. He also told me that he was not married and he'd never had sex. These were very serious symptoms of a very deep-rooted problem. But in spite of this I thought: 'Ah! I shall succeed where others have failed.' Unfortunately, it was not to be. He attended four further sessions before deciding that the treatment wasn't having any effect on his speech problem. Far from being disappointed, he seemed quite pleased. No doubt he's visited other therapists since he saw me.

TEN

Starting therapy; enquiries

To say that most, if not all, people are neurotic to some extent may sound a sweeping statement, but I believe this to be so. How does one define neurosis? I would define it as an imbalance in the mind which may lead to conflict. Some people are able to recognise this in themselves and do something about it. Others may recognise it but would rather leave it alone, not daring to seek help and face the underlying problems. Others again may not be able to recognise any problems at all in themselves. I have met people socially who, once they discover that I'm a psychotherapist, reassure me (or themselves?) that they have no neurotic problems. And if any suggestion is made that some action of theirs may be neurotic, they become very angry. This is an indication of strong resistance to finding out about themselves.

Having decided to do something about your problem, how do you find a good therapist?

The British Hypnotherapy Association, 67 Upper Berkeley Street, London W1H 7DH, the best treatment and referral organisation, maintains a register of practitioners who have had at least four years of training in psychotherapy and hypnotherapy. Write to them, stating your problem, your age, and any treatments you are having or have had. If you work in an area other than where you live, state in what area. Enclose £1. You will then be sent a pamphlet answering the usual questions, plus details on the nearest registered psychotherapists likely to be available and suitable. Their fees will be stated.

But what if you can't afford to see a psychotherapist privately, or there isn't one on the register in your area?

You could visit your general medical practitioner and ask him to refer you to someone. Not many medical practitioners know much about emotional problems or psychotherapy, but he may know of someone who has had some relevant training. He may, of course, believe that psychotherapy is to do with psychiatry, and refer you to a psychiatrist. Or he may himself dabble in psychotherapy, for better or worse. Usually, GP's recognise that they have not had relevant training and if you have an emotional problem they simply fob you off with drugs, which cannot resolve the problem and may create new ones, but might temporarily suppress the symptom.

Your local library or town hall or Citizens' Advice Bureau may be able to put you onto a local psychotherapy place.

Some therapists advertise. But if a psychotherapist or hypnotherapist is any good he shouldn't need to advertise. If he does, he isn't on the register of the British Hypnotherapy Association, and probably has had little or no relevant training.

In any event, it is wise to decide for yourself the competence of any professional person you consult, and psychotherapists are no exception. Is he honest? Does he have integrity? Does he mean what he says? Do you think he will put you first, rather than any theoretical dogma he has been indoctrinated with? You will need to choose wisely, or you may waste a lot of time and money without getting anywhere.

The consultation
Having made enquiries and received details of treatment as well as details of practitioners available, the next step is to arrange a consultation. Some people cannot get any further than the enquiry; they back down at the last minute. I have answered the phone to enquirers who would not give their name or address, which suggested that they were very hostile or paranoid, or too frightened to go any further. Some enquirers ring up to have a bash at the therapist, to give vent to aggressive feelings. This kind of time-waster is a nuisance, having to be dealt with firmly, otherwise the therapist becomes a punch-bag which, unless he is a masochist, he will not choose to accept.

Although hypnosis can be very useful in helping patients sort their problems out, it does also attract people who want an instant cure, believing that hypnosis is a panacea. This is usually an infantile wish, an expectation of magic. In spite of explanations of what is involved, many people won't accept that hypnosis is simply an aid to treatment, not a treatment in itself. Realistic enquirers, however, are sincere and easy to deal with.

You may consult a therapist working on his own, or you may consult someone working as part of an organisation of therapists. An advantage of dealing with an organisation of therapists is that you may get a choice of practitioner. More important, the organisation may be one which insists on adequate standards of training, ensures ethical standards and sees that its practitioners maintain a competent level of treatment.

Also, if you aren't satisfied with your therapist, you can change to someone else. The choice will usually include a scale of fees. Fees should be related to the experience of the therapist, what his overheads are and how much time he'll allocate per session. Normally, a therapist working in a large city will charge more than someone working in the country. Locality of the practitioner is important. The nearer the practitioner, the less time and money the patient spends on travelling. Yet in spite of the practical advantages of seeing someone locally, some patients prefer to come up to London. Working in London, I have had patients come to see me from Birmingham, Bristol and Portsmouth. Many people believe that by coming up to London, they are seeing a better practitioner than they would in the country. Likewise with fees. If a therapist doesn't charge enough, it may be thought that he isn't any good. Some patients, apart from believing they are receiving better treatment, find it easier travelling up to London, rather than going across country to visit a therapist.

Even after having made an appointment for a consultation, many patients still have difficulty in getting to the consulting-room. Some patients oversleep or forget the appointment altogether; others may get lost on the way, or go to the wrong address. These kinds of people don't usually make good patients, even if they do manage to start treatment. Being late for a session, especially the consultation, is usually a bad sign. Sometimes patients are so late that they miss the appointment altogether. Sessions normally last 50 minutes (the 50-minute hour), and I can remember one patient arriving for her consultation exactly 50 minutes late.

This is one reason for collecting fees in advance. If a

session has not been paid for and the patient doesn't turn up, the therapist may lose his fee and the patient is not being helped. Often the fact that the patient has paid for the appointment induces him to turn up.

Most patients, however, arrive on time or a little early and are co-operative. With experience, a therapist chooses what kind of patient he takes on. The therapist should use his time to the best advantage, taking on patients he can help most. There is no point in taking on a patient who is going to be difficult and if there is doubt whether he can be helped, if there are other patients who could be using the same time to greater benefit.

If you see a good therapist he will insist on certain terms and conditions regarding your treatment. This is important as, apart from avoiding any misunderstanding, it gives the patient a justified sense of security. It indicates that the therapist is genuine and that the patient has to take the treatment seriously. If a patient comes to see me, he must first agree to the conditions of coming and pay his consultation fee. He can then arrange an appointment. This ensures that the patient knows what is involved as well as protecting me from time-wasters and trouble-makers. Agreed conditions are especially important if hypnosis is used as many people are ill-informed yet have dogmatic ideas about hypnosis.

The consultation is one of the most important parts of therapy. The patient is making an important decision and probably a difficult one. It probably has taken him a lot of courage and determination to make it to the consulting-room. He may have been putting it off for years. He is entrusting the therapist with intimate aspects of his life.

The therapist, on the other hand, has to decide whether he is able to help the patient and if his treatment is the most suitable. He has to decide if he is the best person to help the patient. Would it be better if the patient saw another practitioner? If the therapist decides to take on the patient, he has to assess how often the patient should attend. This is one of the most important decisions he has to make after having decided to take on the patient. Is once a week enough? Should it be two, three or perhaps five times a week? Some therapists make the mistake of not seeing a patient often enough. The therapist may feel guilty if he thinks the patient hasn't enough money, but it's unethical for the therapist to compromise, risking a probability that the treatment will not succeed. The therapist has to decide if he can help the patient and, if so, how often the patient should attend. Having decided this, the therapist has to remain firm. If the patient cannot afford to see a particular therapist, he must go elsewhere.

Some therapists allow the patient to manipulate them. Once this happens the therapy is unlikely to succeed, with the patient prematurely terminating treatment. The therapist should view the case quite objectively, having the interest of the patient at heart. This may entail giving the patient not what he wants, but what he needs. If the therapist decides that the patient needs daily treatment, he should say so, being firm, not allowing himself to be persuaded to change his mind. If the therapy is on a phoney basis, it's not only unethical, but it's wasting the patient's time and money.

Unfortunately, too many therapists haven't sorted out their own problems, with the consequence of not being objective enough regarding their patients. Some therapists unwittingly allow themselves to be mentally seduced by attractive patients, giving them what they want. Some therapists feel hostile towards older patients, seeing them as parent-figures. This countertransference is a very important aspect of psychotherapy, sometimes overlooked by the therapist may have. Any therapist should be aware of any feelings he has towards a patient. The patient, after all, is an easy target for any neurosis the therapist may have. Many people take up the profession simply to act out their own neuroses on their patients, even if they aren't aware of what they are doing. It's only too easy for a sadistic therapist to exploit a masochistic patient.

At the end of the consultation the patient has to decide whether he wants to embark on treatment. The majority of patients don't return after a consultation. There are various reasons for this. Some patients, having made the effort to attend a consultation, are too frightened to go ahead with treatment. They would rather live with their neuroses than face their problems. Others come with misguided ideas as to what is involved in therapy, becoming annoyed and disheartened when they realise that their childish wish for an instant cure will not be gratified. All prospective patients who contact The Psychotherapy Centre are sent information about treatment, but some don't bother to read it carefully, giving it a cursory glance. Some patients I have come across have thrown it away, having then to ask for a further copy.

Some patients test the practitioner, hoping in some way to expose a weakness, which they will then exploit. Some female patients flirt, hoping to seduce the therapist either physically or mentally. When he doesn't respond, they get annoyed and walk out. One female patient, to whom I was giving a consultation, told me with great relish that she had seduced her physician. At the end of the consultation, she requested late evening appointments, hoping to seduce me in a similar manner to her physician. After one or two sessions, when she realised she wasn't going to succeed, she stopped coming.

There are patients who offer the therapist a cheque without a banker's card, hoping he'll accept it, which would give the patient the opportunity to cancel the cheque. This kind of patient wants to vent his hostile feelings, which probably originated with his parents, on the therapist.

Some patients appear very keen to commence treatment, making and paying for further appointments at the end of their consultation. Then, a day or two later, they ring up to cancel their appointments. This is often due to discussing treatment with a friend or relative who has put them off. At this stage, patients are very vulnerable, perhaps having doubts as to whether they are doing the right thing, becoming influenced by others. One of the conditions that patients see me on is that they do not discuss treatment with anybody else at the start of therapy. Coming for therapy is a personal decision which the patient himself must make. Unfortunately, people who want others to tell them what to do, like a child obeying a parent, only too often find people who are willing to tell them what to do.

This kind of patient is among those who have never been allowed by their parents to make decisions, always relying on being told what to do. Often, other people feel threatened if they know that a friend or relative is going for therapy. They feel: 'If there's something wrong with him, then there might be something wrong with me.'

Many people do, however, decide to embark on treatment. Often, some of their acquaintances, seeing the results, decide to have therapy themselves.

Patients can often sense what the practitioner feels. Sometimes a practitioner might be eager to take on a patient, trying to ensure at the consultation that he returns. This anxiety may be felt by the patient, who might be made to feel that the practitioner is unsure about his abilities, which could put the patient off. Some practitioners feel rejected if the patient doesn't return.

I remember one woman who came to see me because she had the nervous habit of pulling her hair out. She expected an instant cure with hypnosis, but I explained that she needed psychotherapy, not suggestion treatment. She was a bad case, which didn't make me keen to take her on. At the end of the consultation she decided that she would not proceed with treatment. Inwardly I gave a sigh of relief. She must have sensed this, because she immediately changed her mind, wanting to make a further appointment.

Good practitioners, who have had sufficient therapy themselves to sort out their problems, are aware of any feelings they may have towards their patients, not allowing these feelings to affect the therapy adversely.

ELEVEN

The therapeutic situation
One-to-one psychodynamic psychotherapy depends largely for its efficacy on transference; transference of feelings by the patient onto the therapist. Usually these are feelings which the patient has towards his parents, orginating in the parent/child relationship. Transference is a phenomenon experienced by everyone, to a larger or lesser extent, in everyday life. In getting married, for instance, you would transfer feelings from your father to your husband or from your mother to your wife.

In the therapeutic situation this transference is exaggerated, mainly by the therapist being objective, not becoming directly involved with the patient. The therapist remains an enigma, an unknown quantity to the patient, who sees in the therapist attributes which belonged to one of the patient's parents and originated in an earlier period of the life of the patient. In the therapeutic situation the patient sees the therapist as his father or his mother or both. The sex of the therapist is not of great consequence, as the patient will see him in one or both sexual roles.

The therapeutic situation allows parent/child problems to be re-enacted in the therapy, which enables the patient to work through feelings which no longer apply. The therapist is a catalyst, allowing the patient to respond to the situation. Any reaction by the patient is then investigated by the therapist. In therapy, especially if hypnosis is successfully used, hidden feelings surface; forgotten events become conscious. The situation enables the patient to expose his thoughts and feelings, being able to express himself to the therapist without criticism or censorship.

Sometimes the transference by the patient can be expressed quite dramatically. A 47-year-old widow came to see me because she had various problems, which included depression and a hatred of men. Her husband's death had made her feel guilty, as she believed she was responsible for it, although she could not substantiate this with any evidence. It was solely a figment of her imagination. This guilt could be traced back to her hatred of her father and her wish to kill him.

She was afraid of trying hypnosis as she thought she would lose control of herself. Eventually, after having attended a number of sessions, she agreed to be hypnotised. She had always insisted on sitting in a chair facing me, rather than lying on the couch. It was in this sitting position that I hypnotised her. She appeared to have a good response but, when I asked her to say what was on her mind, she blurted out:

'No! No! You won't!'

She then opened her eyes, being very upset and tearful. She told me that she had been very afraid.

'I saw your face,' she said, 'it was my father's.'

On another occasion a young male patient told me, in hypnosis, the following:

'I'm scared and frightened of you. You might be getting bored again. It's deliberate on your part. Father didn't listen to what I said. He wasn't interested. I would like to go over and cry on my father's lap. He might say: "I understand you." ' (The patient then started crying.) 'If I could just let go on his lap.'

At another session, the same patient told me:

'The way I see my father affects how I see other people.'

The transference that the patient has on the therapist may be positive or negative or, more correctly, a predominantly positive or negative transference, as there are always both feelings present. These are feelings of love and hate which the patient was towards his parents. A patient with a positive transference is always easier to treat than one with a negative transference. If a patient has a strong negative transference, it may take a long time to sort out his problems.

Some patients find the therapeutic situation difficult, seeing their hated father or mother in the therapist, something which can give rise to uncomfortable feelings. A patient with a strong negative transference might break off treatment soon after commencing, particularly if he is not attending sessions frequently enough. The feelings of hate may be too strong for the patient to accept. By breaking off, he avoids facing unpleasant facts about himself and punishes the therapist by rejecting him. The more skilful and experienced the practitioner, the better the chances are that a difficult patient will remain in therapy and benefit.

Other patients find the therapeutic situation quite pleasant, enjoying the sessions. These are easy patients, who usually progress well, making the therapist's job equally pleasant and enjoyable.

By the very nature of therapy, any repressed hostile feelings that a patient may have are transferred onto the therapist. These feelings may come out even before the patient has seen the therapist. At one time I allowed patients to book an appointment for a consultation, paying when they arrived. This system worked well to a point, but it failed with very hostile patients, who made appointments then didn't keep them. This can be frustrating for the therapist, who has to waste a session waiting, and enables the patient to act out his neurosis but sacrifice the chance of resolving it.

Even so, this system had the advantage that a patient could make an appointment to see a therapist immediately, providing there was a vacancy. Under the present system I insist that all patients pay for their appointments in advance, which necessitates a wait of ten days if there is a cheque to clear. Some would-be patients are put off if they cannot see someone at once, though this is usually part of their neurosis. But unless a therapist is neurotic, he doesn't want to waste any sessions waiting for patients who don't turn up, unless he has been paid for the time.

Sometimes when a patient is offered an appointment after having had to wait, he will refuse it, demanding his fee back. He may feel resentful that he had to wait and he may have found someone else to see.

Some patients spend a long time gathering enough courage to see a therapist. But then they get upset if they cannot be offered an immediate appointment. This could reflect an infantile desire to have everything at once.

The relationship between therapist and patient is a special one, in which the patient bares his soul while the therapist remains an anonymous observer. Some patients resent this as they feel they aren't getting anything from the therapist. They feel it's a one-way traffic, the patient giving everything to the therapist, while the therapist restricts himself to asking questions.

Some patients complain of not getting any feed-back from the therapist, which could indicate that they weren't emotionally fed by their parents.

The trial period

The first few sessions are perhaps the most crucial in the course of treatment. I always stipulate with new patients when I take them on that there will be a trial period to begin with. This can serve two purposes. One is to discover whether the therapist and patient are suited; the other being that many patients, if immediately accepted by the therapist, express their hostile feelings by rejecting him and breaking off treatment.

During this trial period, the patient may either settle into treatment, progressing well, or he may develop a negative transference, which he may express by discontinuing therapy. At this stage of treatment, the transference of feelings by the patient onto the therapist is taking place. Transference is not always immediate, taking a number of sessions to become established. In this respect, hypnosis can be useful, as it helps the patient to accelerate his transference of feelings. At this period, when the transference is being established, it's crucial for the therapist to be aware of what is happening regarding the patient's feelings. It's vital that any untoward behaviour by the patient is investigated. A difficult patient may begin to feel very hostile, expressing his feelings in negative ways. He may start arriving late for sessions, he may be awkward and argumentative, or he may cancel appointments.

Sometimes the feelings that the patient is beginning to experience, albeit at an unconscious level, may not be acceptable to him. Sometimes therapy progresses rapidly. In some cases this is disturbing for the patient. It must be remembered that some patients can only accept so much emotional change at a time; too much change, too quickly, isn't acceptable. Usually the opposite is the case; change is slow. Many patients are anxious to see improvements, and if there are no immediate signs of any change, they may wonder if they should continue their therapy. This is one time when the frequency of sessions is important. If the patient isn't attending often enough, the gap between sessions may give him time to build up resistance.

At this time, when the patient feels most vulnerable, outside influences may affect him, particularly what people say to him. After all, he is venturing into something completely new, putting his life in the hands of a therapist he may know little about. Some patients believe they should tell their GP. The GP may have some understanding of the problem, encouraging the patient. Or he may be ignorant, telling the patient that he should consult somebody who is medically qualified.

It's important for the patient himself to make the decision to come for treatment, and to commit himself to therapy. Results from treatment are not always immediate and the patient may get worse before getting better. Improvement is usually steady, but sometimes it may involve the patient having ups and downs before recovery is complete.

Patients benefitting from a single session

Occasionally, a patient may come for a consultation only, deriving help from this single visit. Sometimes, just talking to a therapist about problems which have never been mentioned before can be of great benefit to the patient. Very often, patients tell me how relieved they are to talk to someone, getting things off their chest. It's probably the first time they have confided in anybody. Patients usually find that it's much easier to confide in a therapist who is a stranger and objective, rather than in a friend or relative who may want to give advice or even be critical.

One patient who did benefit enormously from a single visit was a 25-year-old Swedish girl who made an appointment to see me because she had become involved with a married man who had separated from his wife. The patient told me that the man had lost interest in her but she was still infatuated with him. This was a problem, as she wanted to go back to Sweden but found that she couldn't leave the man.

She also told me that she lacked confidence when with people, which produced panic feelings in her. If she was going out in the evening on a social engagement, she would have to have a couple of drinks to give herself confidence. She said her father was an unemotional man, strict and dominant, yet she felt that he was insecure. When he got angry, instead of expressing himself he would go completely silent. Her lack of confidence had started around puberty, but had got worse during the last three years.

At the end of the consultation I told her that I would take her on as a patient, seeing her twice a week. She asked to make a further appointment, but some days later she rang to cancel it, saying that she had decided to return to Sweden.

This patient had a lot of problems which originated in her childhood, probably mostly to do with a lack of good relationship with her father. I told her at the consultation that these problems needed sorting out, which would have entailed a considerable amount of therapy. Although she did not embark on therapy, her one visit enabled her to get away from the man she was infatuated with, and to return to Sweden, which was the purpose of her coming in the first place.

Another patient who benefitted from a single visit was a young married woman who came to see me for a sexual problem. At the consultation it emerged that she had many other problems which needed sorting out. I decided to take her on as a patient, and she decided to start therapy, making a further appointment. When she came for her next visit, she told me with pleasure that she had stopped smoking after the consultation, without making any conscious effort. At the consultation she hadn't mentioned the fact that she smoked.

TWELVE

Young patients and their parents and relatives
Sometimes a patient in her late teens or early twenties (usually it's a girl) will come to a consultation accompanied by a parent, usually her mother. This is invariably a bad sign. If the parent cannot let a daughter or son of this age come to a consultation alone, it indicates that the patient has a possessive, over-protective parent. Some parents even want to accompany their offspring into the consulting-room.

It's important for the therapist to be on the patient's side, even if the parents are paying for the therapy. The patient must be able to feel that the therapist understands his problem, is willing to listen, and will treat what is said as confidential. This is particularly true with children and young adults who are still financially dependent on their parents. Many parents will not listen to their children; many parents aren't interested in them.

Sometimes, if a parent takes a child to a specialist who is in private practice, he will pay attention to the parent who is paying his fee instead of to the patient. This happened to one of my patients, a girl of 17, who was taken by her mother to a Harley Street physician because the girl had back trouble. This patient told me that the physician never addressed a word to her, giving all his time to the mother, who was enjoying the attention she was receiving.

Occasionally, a parent will ring up the Centre or call

at the door, wanting information for an offspring. They appear to be doing the best for their daughter or son, but it is often only a phoney concern. Often it turns out that the offspring is in his mid-twenties, old enough to look after himself. We always tell the enquirer that the person needing treatment must contact us himself. This is always therapeutically beneficial to the patient; he feels more independent and less pressurised by his parents.

Some parents are keen for their offspring to have therapy, being pleased if the symptoms are cleared up. But some parents don't like it if their offspring start showing signs of independence. As most problems go back to the parent/child relationship, the patient will gradually see his parents as they are and not as he was brought up to believe they were. As many young patients don't earn any money, the parents holding the purse-strings, they can stop the treatment at any time they wish. This is likely to happen when the patient begins to think for himself, the parents feeling they are losing their hold over their child.

One such case was a female, aged 22 years, who came to see me as she had a slight speech impediment which affected her career (she was training to be a teacher). She was also overweight, by about 1½ stone. Over a period of about three years she had been to see a speech therapist, a spiritual healer and a hypnotist. None of these people had helped her. She told me that she had sex with her boyfriend at week-ends, but she couldn't get an orgasm. She also was a strict vegetarian. When she went to see the hypnotist, he'd used tactile induction, the session lasting three hours. She said she hadn't trusted him, which was why she hadn't gone back to him.

The patient's mother came with her on the first visit, waiting in the reception room during the consultation. When I asked the patient why her mother had come, she replied that her mother didn't want anything 'untoward' to happen. On the patient's next visit, her mother appeared again. When I again asked the patient why, she said her mother had to come up to the West End to do some shopping. She then told me that she didn't like the questions I'd asked her at the consultation about sex. She also told me a dream in which she was being chased by two bulls. At the following session she told me a dream about a house on fire and some children jumping out of a window to escape. At the end of the session she made a further appointment, but some days later she rang to cancel it without giving a reason. I concluded that her mother had a very tight hold on her daughter and, although she wanted her daughter to improve, she didn't want her to become independent. The patient was also frightened of her own sexual feelings, which may have had to do with her relationship with her father, feelings which she transferred to the various therapists she'd seen. It was probably a case of wanting to have sex with her father and therefore her therapist, while at the same time feeling very guilty about it.

Sometimes, people, especially relatives, actively interfere with the patient's therapy. One patient of mine, an unmarried female of 25, was seeing me to get over her anxiety, lack of confidence, and depression. She made rapid progress, starting to express her aggressive feelings, particularly towards her sister who bullied her, as well as getting herself a boyfriend and having regular sex for the first time in her life, which she thoroughly enjoyed. She had only been coming for a few weeks when her married sister rang the Centre wanting to speak to me. She told me that I ought to know that her sister (the patient) was becoming very aggressive and disturbing the family. I asked her how this could be, as the patient lived on her own, not with her sister. I added that patients have ups and downs before recovery is complete. The patient later told me that her sister didn't like her standing up for herself, speaking her mind. I concluded that the patient's sister was herself much in need of psychotherapy.

It's always preferable for a patient to pay for his own treatment. There's more incentive for him to recover if he is making a financial sacrifice himself. If someone else is paying, there's not the same incentive. It may be advisable in some cases for a young patient to wait until he is able to afford to pay for his own treatment rather than risk his parents paying for therapy only to withdraw their financial support when the patient begins to recover and show signs of independence.

In some cases the young patient may use therapy to get his own back on his parents. He may use the treatment as a weapon to punish his parents by the parents paying out large sums of money for his treatment without any beneficial results.

One patient who fell into this category was a man of 20, who was suffering from 'bad nerves' since he'd gone up to university, where he wasn't able to complete his studies. He suffered from depression, having a feeling of unreality. He admitted that he hadn't got on with his fellow students.

His father was a weak, unemotional man, with whom the patient had no emotional contact. His mother was also unemotional, but she had a stronger personality than his father. The patient also had a sister, four years younger than himself. It wasn't a happy family.

I agreed to take him on as a patient, seeing him twice a week. As he worked in a bookshop, which didn't pay very much, his parents helped him financially, which eventually resulted in him attending five sessions a week, his parents paying the greater part of his fees. He progressed to begin with, but progress became slower as time went on. He eventually settled into a routine of attending promptly five times a week, but not making any further progress. He was using me as a substitute parent, getting my time and attention. At the same time he was punishing his parents by taking their money but not deriving any benefit from therapy. I eventually told him that if by a given date he hadn't progressed sufficiently I would terminate therapy. There was no significant change by the due date, so the therapy was terminated.

Sometimes it can be a problem for a therapist to decide whether treatment is cost-effective. In this case it wasn't. I suggested to this patient that he could try to see someone else. Sometimes a change of practitioner helps; a different approach or a different personality may do the trick.

Nowadays, although I take on patients of 16 and over, I'm not keen on taking on any young patient who is not financially self-sufficient. I have in the past taken on children and, although they have benefitted, the parents, usually the mother, interfered sooner or later, withdrawing their child from therapy. I have also taken on a child whose mother was in therapy with another practitioner, which theoretically should be viable. But, unless the mother is sufficiently sorted out, the inevitable happens, and the child is taken away from therapy. Nowadays, like the other practitioners at The Psychotherapy Centre, I insist that the parents must first have therapy before sending along their child. Invariably, the parents need therapy and invariably their children benefit from the parents sorting themselves out.

Couples seeking therapy
Sometimes a husband sends his wife for treatment, or a wife persuades her husband to have therapy. This kind of patient is seldom a promising case. Quite often a husband will blame his wife if the marriage isn't working, and she blames him. Sex problems are often a bone of contention in marriages or sexual relationships, one partner blaming the other for any failures in bed. Masters and Johnson claim over 50% of marriages are unsound because of psychosexual problems. Most emotional problems affect sexual performance, and unless a marriage is successful in bed there's little chance of it being successful anywhere else.

I have found that it's imperative in all cases, except children, that the patient himself seeks therapy, not being persuaded, bullied, cajoled, blackmailed or dragged along to the consulting room by someone else. Whether it's a parent, a close relation, a lover, a husband or a wife, it's never a healthy sign if a prospective patient arrives for a consultation with someone else; I then have little expectation that the patient will embark on therapy.

One man was persuaded by his wife to seek treatment because he had some emotional problems which were affecting his marriage. He admitted during the consultation that he was often impotent with his wife, particularly when she got sexually aroused. He was 36 years old and had been married for ten years, a marriage which had produced four children. He was a reluctant patient and progress was slow. After about forty sessions his repressed homosexual feelings started to manifest themselves in dreams.

He wasn't consciously aware of these feelings, but he stopped treatment, saying that he had gone as far as he could in therapy, adding that his wife should come instead, rationalising that many of his problems were caused by his wife's behaviour. As I have already mentioned, patients with repressed homosexual desires often break off therapy rather than face their hidden feelings.

His wife did attend, coming for about 14 sessions. She was a much better patient than her husband, being more co-operative and outgoing, deriving great benefit from her visits. She admitted that she was the dominant partner in the marriage.

The main fault lay with the husband, as the lack of sex made his wife very frustrated, which resulted in her getting irritated with him, making his sexual impotence worse. In spite of knowing that his impotence was the main cause of their problem, he still wanted his wife to receive treatment as he rationalised that her attitude made him impotent. He, unconsciously, saw her as his bossy mother, while his wife saw him as her weak, dominated father. This was a case where the sexual roles were reversed, the woman being dominant and the man being subservient. In cases of marital problems, it's best that both parties receive treatment, preferably with different therapists. In the particular case I've just quoted, it was not a good sign that the wife got her husband to come for therapy. Unless a patient is keen to help himself, treatment isn't likely to be successful.

Other complications can also arise with couples. If one partner goes for therapy he or she may not want the other to know. If a wife goes for therapy (usually it's the wife, as women tend to be more ready to accept that something is wrong and do something about it), she may not want her husband to know. She may feel that she is being unfaithful. After all, her husband may see the therapist as a competitor, another lover. He may object to his wife telling a complete stranger all their marital secrets, or he may object to his wife getting so much attention. Similar difficulties can arise if it's the man who is going for therapy. If one partner goes for treatment it often produces strong jealousy feelings in the other.

In theory, a husband or wife having therapy may decide that their marriage was a mistake. Anxiety in the partner on this score is understandable. After all, people do change in effective psychotherapy, and sometimes they find themselves attracted to different types of people from before. In fact, however, my patients have, as a result of their therapy, tended to get on better with people generally as they become less neurotic, though there can be some difficulties while they are changing. Their marriages, in common with most of their relationships, have improved.

There are neurotic 'therapists', of course, who act out their own problems through their patients, destroying relationships. This is one reason why all reputable psychotherapy organisations insist on their therapists having extensive therapy themselves first of all. The best psychotherapy organisations also ask patients to report long-term results, minimising the risk of patients being referred to dud therapists.

If a patient goes through a stormy time in marriage or

with parents or friends this can, however, be a sign of much-needed self-assertion.

I once had a patient whose husband abruptly terminated her treatment. She was 31 years old, and came to see me because she blushed, which in public attracted people's attention. This she found humiliating. She told me that her marriage was all right and that they had a three-year-old son. However, on further questioning she admitted that she was no longer attracted to her husband, their sex life having petered out. (I find that some patients don't always tell the truth, some being used to dissimulation, saying that things are all right when they aren't.) Her parents had divorced when she was three years old, her mother having custody.

At the consultation, the patient said that she could probably manage to come twice a week, but she didn't want her husband to find out that she was coming for treatment. This might be difficult, she said, as her husband was indirectly paying for therapy, and he wouldn't approve of her having treatment.

She attended two subsequent sessions, in both of which I used hypnosis, to which she had a good response, although she wasn't entirely convinced that she was in hypnosis. This was in spite of her right arm rising at my suggestion. She arranged a further appointment but, shortly before she was expected, her husband rang to say that his wife was cancelling the appointment and not coming any longer. Did he feel threatened by his wife having treatment?

In another case, the patient's boyfriend developed symptoms and became hostile towards me as the patient improved in therapy. She was a 45-year-old divorced American, who came to see me as she was having problems with her boyfriend, who wasn't being faithful to her. She was terrified of rejection, needing a constant, faithful boyfriend. She couldn't get an orgasm with him, but she'd had orgasms with previous boyfriends. She told me that she always needed a man around, she couldn't do without one. She was quite obsessive about this, although she spent a lot of time arguing and fighting with her boyfriend. After coming regularly for about two years, she found that she no longer had this obsession. This was part of her overall improvement. It led to her not being so reliant on her boyfriend. She told me:

'Paul said that he had lost his control over me. My improvement in therapy is making him worse. He's now got a stomach ulcer, he's become impotent and has back pain.'

At another session she said:

'Ever since I've not got angry with Paul, he's not liked it. He doesn't know how to deal with the new me. He calls you a witch-doctor, and wants to know what your credentials are. He doesn't like me getting better.'

Luckily, this patient was financially independent of her boyfriend, paying for her own therapy. Although he objected to her having treatment, he couldn't do anything about it. He felt threatened by the changes that took place in his girlfriend, although he was likely to benefit from them.

THIRTEEN

Patients expressing their feelings to their parents
A difficult task which many patients encounter in their therapy is expressing repressed feelings to their parents. Yet in most cases this is crucial for the patient to be able to recover from his problem.

One's attitude to people generally depends largely on one's attitude to one's parents. A good relationship with the parents will enable one to have good relationships with people generally later in life. Likewise, a bad relationship with parents will lead to bad relationships with other people. Because this relationship between parents and children is so fundamental to one's well-being, it is imperative that patients should be able to express their feelings freely to their parents.

Some therapists believe that patients should tackle these conflicts only in the consulting room. Why? Could it be that these therapists feel guilty about their feelings to their own parents?

Much of therapy is spent enabling patients to express themselves freely. Most people with neurotic problems have had many of their natural outlets for feelings repressed in childhood by their parents. Often, any feelings that the child may have towards its parents which are not acceptable to them are repressed.

Many patients find the thought of expressing their true feelings to their parents a frightening and disturbing thought. This is not surprising. Many people believe that you should be grateful to your parents for bringing you up, perhaps for making financial sacrifices, for paying to send you to school and so on. This attitude is reinforced by some parents and by establishment attitudes. The Church, for example, reinforces this belief by stating that you should honour your father and mother, but not mentioning that you should honour your children.

If you have been brought up to believe that all your parents have done for you was in your own interest, it's difficult to turn round and blame them for your hang-ups. Nevertheless, it is true that many parents do screw up their children, usually without realising it. Some parents excuse themselves by pointing out that they themselves had a deprived childhood, so that they are not to blame. The answer to that is that they should have taken out their frustrations on their own parents, instead of taking them out on their children.

Children, all too often, are the victims of their parents' neuroses. Children are easy targets, especially when they are at a very dependent stage early in their lives. Children are vulnerable and a soft option for parents who cannot express their feelings in the right direction.

Some people have no difficulty in criticising their parents, telling them home truths. Although this may be commendable, inasmuch as feelings are being expressed, it's not sufficient in itself. The aim should not be parent-bashing. There has to be insight. One has to understand what's going on. In addition, there are feelings of love as well as hate. Often, by expressing feelings of hate, feelings of love emerge. This is often manifest in lovers who squabble, then make up, feeling closer together in the end. It can be all too easy to disown one's parents, but this won't solve the basic problems. Usually, the patient's relationship with his parents actually improves once the patient is frank and open with them. Sometimes this helps the parents, and may change them in a way they appreciate.

In virtually all analytic cases, problems relate to a bad parent/child relationship. There are a few exceptions, where problems don't relate back to parents, as in the example I gave of the woman who suffered from cat phobia.

All too often, especially in middle- and upper-class families, children are brought up to be polite and subservient to their elders. This leads to dissimulation, saying things which are not true. It can result in phoney politeness, as well as phoney concern. This will often lead to conflict, doing what is expected by others, against doing what you would like to do. And where there are unexpressed conflicts within you, there are bound to be problems.

Sometimes, patients' own feelings towards their parents come out quite spontaneously. One young female patient told me:

'I had nothing on my mind when I came in here. Now I feel angry, frustrated, and I want to have it out with my parents. If I hadn't come here, I would have thought everything was all right.'

Although she realised, consciously, what she wanted to do, unconsciously she was resistant about going to see her parents. At a later date she told me:

'I was going to go down to see my parents, but a blister developed on my foot. I had to cancel my trip. Then two hours later my foot was OK. It's the same leg which sometimes goes numb or gives me a stiff knee.'

Some patients find it easier to confront their parents than they thought possible. Another young female patient, whose father was dead, told me:

'I had a chat with my mum. I tried to tell her what my feelings were. I was amazed how easy it was. But I felt upset this morning, sad. I think she was a bit shocked.'

Many patients feel very guilty about their aggressive feelings towards their parents. Sometimes, talking to parents can be to the patient's material advantage as well as being therapeutically beneficial. This last patient I have quoted told me a week later:

'I saw my mother on Sunday. She was different. Being very nice. She gave me her piano, which I've always wanted.'

Many patients find that when they become frank with their parents their guilt feelings are alleviated. One middle-aged patient told me:

'Some good came out of seeing my father. I'm not feeling so guilty. I started calling my father Dad.'

Sometimes parents are co-operative, being pleased that their offspring has become more frank. It can alleviate the parents' guilt feelings. One patient, a woman in her thirties, told me:

'I went to see my father. I told him I was coming here for psychotherapy. He told me that he was the cause of my trouble. He said he had always put me down. He thinks that my coming up here is the best thing I've ever done.'

Quite often, parents believe that their children's bad behaviour is innate. This is a convenient rationalisation which allows the parent to avoid the unpleasant truth. One American patient who consulted me firmly believed at the beginning of her therapy that her parents hadn't loved her because she had been a difficult child, and that she had been born this way.

Another patient, a man in his twenties, not only

benefitted enormously by speaking frankly to his parents but it also helped them, especially the father. The patient told me:

'I went to see my parents last night. I got a lot off my chest. I told them they didn't confide in me. They blamed me for this. I told them I was coming here for treatment. Mother didn't like that at all. Father said that I was tricked into seeking revenge on them. I was going to see them on Sunday, but I put it off to last night. During the day I had all these symptoms. Firstly I forgot my keys. Then I got a horrible headache, my stomach was upset and I got pains. The physical symptoms got worse and worse. I had to go home at three o'clock. Last night I asked father why he didn't talk about things to mother. After I'd spoken, they seemed to talk more to each other. Sometimes it would take two weeks before father talked about something that was bothering him.'

A couple of months later he reported:

'I went to see my parents on Sunday. It's important to get things off my mind. It's important to see my parents every week. They've now taken an interest in psychotherapy. My father is getting more aggressive towards mother. They're also getting more generous. They offered to buy me a moped.

'My therapy has helped my father. He's been unlocked. He's much happier. He's doing what he wants to do. He's made new friends. Mother doesn't mind. My therapy has also helped her. Having sorted things out between them, they're saying things they have never said to each other before.'

Some time later he said:

'I was telling my father about my car. It failed the MOT test. Father said: "Go and buy another car." One thing treatment has done is to make my father very generous.'

At a later session the patient reported:

'It's been a new lease of life for my father since I talked to my parents. Things are talked about which would normally be swept under the carpet.'

Some patients may express their feelings to their parents quite forcibly. In 1979, Tommy Hansen probably made legal history. This American of 25 sued his parents for $350,000, charging them with wilful and wanton neglect of his physical and emotional needs. His lawyer called it 'parental malpractice'. His psychiatrist said the lawsuit would give Hansen 'the opportunity to develop alternative ways of dealing with his rage against his parents'. The judge took the side of the parents, deciding that the lawsuit was 'wholly without merit'. The judge was probably a parent himself. This attitude is prevalent in adults, especially parents, who are ready to condemn children rather than to seek the causes of their own problems. In this last case the mother of Tommy Hansen was reported as saying: 'I don't know why all this has happened to my family, but it has. It's terrible. I'm trying very hard to sort it out. Was it us? Or drugs? Genetics? I don't know. No one does really.' No one? From my research I suspect the parents were at fault, although the mother was not able to realise this or would not want to admit it. Suing his parents, even if successful, would not necessarily solve Tommy's problems. Did he try and talk it out with his parents, expressing his rage verbally, rather than simply wanting to punish them?

FOURTEEN

Results and follow-ups

At what point does therapy terminate? This is a question that will arise sooner or later in the course of treatment. Usually it's the patient who decides to stop therapy. Sometimes the therapist will make the decision, and occasionally therapy ceases by mutual consent.

There are many reasons why treatment comes to an end. When can one assess that a patient is 'cured'? I use that word with caution as the therapist can't always know for certain that the patient has sorted himself out sufficiently to be able to live a full, successful life. The usual question that the practitioner has to ask himself is: 'Has the patient attained his full potential?'

Many patients come to therapy with a particular problem, the presenting symptom, which, once resolved, may make the patient feel that he can discontinue. However, during treatment other problems often come to light, problems which the patient was not aware of. Many patients do not realise how much of their behaviour is neurotic. The therapist should try to continue their treatment as long as is necessary to resolve the remaining problems – as long as is practically possible while the patient is benefitting.

Some patients break off prematurely, not resolving all their problems, while others, if they are seeing an incompetent therapist, may continue therapy for a long time without gaining any benefits. The length of treatment can vary enormously, from one session to many years. The efficacy of treatment depends mainly on the response by the patient. Obviously, a good therapist is essential for satisfactory results, but basically the speed and good results of the therapy will depend largely on how well the patient responds to the treatment as well as on the nature of the causes of the problem. However good a therapist is, some patients, because of the nature of their problems and their mental make-up, cannot be helped. Conversely, even with a mediocre therapist, a good patient will often recover quickly from his problems. A good happy childhood is an indication that the patient will have a good response to treatment, resolving his problems quickly. While a bad, unhappy childhood would indicate the opposite: a bad response and a lengthy treatment.

However, there are exceptions. I have had patients who have had a traumatic childhood, yet responded well to treatment, deriving great benefit.

In what ways can one tell how effective the therapy has been? Obviously the therapist is guided by both what he can see for himself and by what the patient tells him during the therapy. But this is not sufficient. Follow-ups are essential to establish how good the therapy was and what the long-term effects are. After therapy terminates, follow-ups should be made over a number of years. This is the only reliable way of determining the long-term effects of the treatment.

Some practitioners claim results and many believe these claims are true. But unless they check up on how the patient is a year after finishing therapy, and periodically after that, they do not know whether any benefits were only temporary. Some hypnotists make extravagant claims regarding their success in stopping people smoking. But many patients who stop smoking start again after a time. Hypnosis can be very useful in helping smokers, but it may only have a temporary effect. If smoking is only a habit the result may be permanent, but if smoking is a neurotic symptom, the desire to smoke again is likely to return.

Many practitioners believe they have helped their patients, when they don't actually know. It's easy to claim a success without doing a thorough follow-up. One example was a patient who came to see me because she was frightened of people vomiting. She avoided such places as pubs, where there was a possibility of someone being sick. She found that this phobia impaired her social life as well as being an embarrassment. She told me that she had been to a well-known London hospital where they specialise in behaviour therapy, especially for cases of phobia. She stated that the treatment involved being shown pictures of people being sick, to accustom her to these sights. She said that she had dreaded going to the hospital as this form of treatment terrified her, in addition to which the treatment was useless. At the end of the course she told them she had been cured. She felt she couldn't face any more of the treatment and she believed that she would have had a nervous breakdown if she'd continued. She added that the treatment had made her worse, not better. No follow-up attempts were made by the hospital. There is little doubt that she was marked up as a successful case.

One problem with follow-ups is to trace patients once they have terminated therapy. Some change their address; others may want to forget that they went for therapy, however successful the outcome. In Britain, amongst some people, there's still a suspicion of psychological treatment, with a stigma attached to anybody who becomes a psychotherapy patient. Some patients, who have not sorted out all their problems, may still have hostile feelings towards the therapist which were not resolved. That these problems weren't resolved is usually due to the patient terminating therapy prematurely.

I usually send out follow-up letters six months or a year after the patient has stopped seeing me. After that, I try to keep in touch every year or two. Replies can sometimes by very revealing. I have had patients who had thought that they made little progress in therapy, but, after having terminated therapy, have replied to my follow-up letter saying that they have made big strides in their lives, not thinking of attributing their changes to therapy.

One such patient was a married woman of 26, who came to see me for an overweight problem which she'd had since puberty. At the age of 18, still unmarried, she became pregnant and, not wanting the baby, had an abortion. When she came to see me she was married, but had no children. Although she said she was happily married, her husband, who was a publican, had outbursts of temper. She helped her husband in the pub, but she didn't enjoy the work. Her relationship with her parents had not been good and her mother at one time had been near to having a nervous breakdown.

The patient attended two further sessions after the consultation. We used hypnosis, into which she went easily. But she cancelled her fourth appointment, saying her husband was ill. She never made any further appointments. A year later I wrote to her to enquire how helpful her visits were, as well as to find out how she was getting on. She replied from a different address, saying:

'Unfortunately, I did not find my visits to you very helpful and that was the reason why I did not continue. However, my circumstances have changed dramatically in the last six months. I have an interesting new job and a wonderful boyfriend. Although I haven't overcome my problem entirely, I am so much happier that it doesn't worry me any more.'

Some patients don't realise the benefits of therapy until some time after they have stopped treatment. Only in retrospect can they credit therapy for any improvement in their life. One patient who fitted this category was a 44-year-old married man who said he was under strain, being emotionally confused, with blocks and difficulties. He'd not had sex with his wife for eighteen months, and they'd had it only infrequently before that. His wife didn't enjoy sex. He didn't get on with his father, while his mother hadn't shown him any affection.

He attended six sessions before abruptly discontinuing, breaking off with a negative transference. About six months later I wrote to him to enquire how he was progressing and how helpful his sessions were. He replied as follows:

'Since seeing you I have gone through periods of mental disarray as well as greater understanding of myself. The result is that I am beginning to see myself as an independent individual, special to myself, with much capacity and far more intelligence than I had given myself credit for. I feel therefore that my short time under your influence has been of dramatic benefit.

'At the time, though, I did not like it. I felt offended

and disorientated. The sequence of memories seemed unstructured and the lack of diagnosis, discussion between us, or informed explanations confused me.

'This lack of sense of identification bewildered me. From your literature I had expected to receive "pills" rather as one expects from the doctor for some illness or complaint. That there would be an "operation" and I would feel better. Instead I felt worse and this disheartened me.'

I was interested to note that he had expected a quick cure from reading the literature he had been sent. The literature we send to enquirers is very clear as to what is involved in therapy, with no mention of instant cures. As I have written elsewhere in this book, some enquirers don't read the literature sent them, or they completely misconstrue what is written, to fit their own preconceived ideas as to what is involved.

These two examples were of patients who only came for a few sessions, then broke off with strong negative feelings. Other patients fully realise the value of therapy, attending regularly until they have sorted their problems out, irrespective as to how long it takes. One such patient was an American woman aged 45, who had been married and divorced twice. She enjoyed sex, but she had no children. She came to see me as she'd encountered a difficulty with her current boyfriend who believed that he'd found someone else and wanted to leave her. This rejection had precipitated a crisis which she didn't think she could cope with. She was living and working in London, but she wanted to go back to the States eventually.

At the age of 25 she'd had group therapy in New York for two years, going twice a week. She said that the therapy had been helpful. (Although later, as she improved, she realised that the therapy had not been of any use.) She came from what she considered a typical New York Jewish family. She did not get on with her parents, who were still living in the States. She was an only child.

I agreed to take her on, wanting to see her twice a week. She turned out to be a good patient, coming regularly and co-operating fully with the therapy. She hardly missed a session, taking her holidays when I took mine. She had her ups and downs, but progress was steady overall. After about two years, she decided that she'd overcome her main problem, that of her fear of being rejected and not having a man in her life. She returned to the States, from where soon after she wrote to me, unsolicited, to tell me how she was getting on. Her letter was a long one, giving details of her progress and her new life. Here are some of the salient comments she made:

'I have only good news to write. I found a lovely, large, bright apartment in my favourite part of Manhattan. I sold my mass-market paperback novel, based on the outline and the first hundred pages, for $10,000 advance against royalties. And I'm in love with a splendid man.

'On my return to New York I felt happy and confident, and things went well from the moment I stepped off the plane.

'In retrospect, I see how much I was programmed to be unhappy and unsuccessful, as punishment for having been a "bad girl" to my parents. Unconsciously I picked mates who fulfilled my neurotic needs.' She wrote that she'd had an opportunity to compare her new man with her ex-husband, as well as with her troublesome man in England.

'The changes in me are enormous. I have lost my feelings of anxiety at being with a man where there is no conflict. Now I welcome the lack of friction. No longer am I tempted to do exactly what a man does not want, to test how far I can go, and to invite rejection. I am no longer dependent or insecure. And far from being attracted to failures, I am now impatient with them and turned off. I even look for more pleasurable reading, rather than immersing myself in the works of the tortured Titans of literature who were primarily trying desperately to transmute their pain into art.

'I no longer take my father's outrageous behaviour seriously. That he could "forget" to congratulate me on selling my book only amused me and told me a lot about his problem.

'What disturbs me, apart from mother's plight, is that I see in her my old self at its very worst. I had several long talks with her, telling her how I had solved several lifelong problems and suggesting some sort of therapy to give her a little more confidence in herself. She kept making excuses and throwing all the blame on my father. *He* doesn't encourage her, *he* won't drive her, *he* won't be happy paying for the therapy, and so forth. She is utterly unwilling to accept responsibility for her own problems. Probably it's too late for her. Nobody can take her by the hand. I'm glad it wasn't too late for me.

'I've been feeling very lucky. Some of my friends have been in therapy for twenty years or more, without a successful resolution of their problems. It's sad to hear them talking about their "shrinks" as if they were as inconsequential as barbers and hairdressers. Also, too many therapists give advice and get chummy with their patients, to an extent that seems antitherapeutic.

My two female therapist friends who, I hope, are competent, view me as a walking phenomenon and rush back to their patients with renewed hope. For once in my life I had the pleasure of hearing a woman say wistfully, "You really know how to pick a man." I think that Errol is special, but however the situation develops with him ultimately, I know that there are successful people out there for me if I want them.

'I am grateful for your patience and skill which were so effective in treating my neuroses. The therapy has really made a difference. Thank you.

'My best wishes to you and others at the Centre in continuing to help their patients realise their potentials.'

This patient was lucky inasmuch as she improved dramatically in less than two hundred sessions. Some patients may spend much longer in therapy without showing such good results. But whatever the outcome of therapy, the only certain way to assess the efficacy of one's treatment is to follow up patients after the termination of therapy, over a number of years.

FIFTEEN

Two cases of hypno-analysis
I shall finish this book by giving two accounts of patients who benefitted enormously from the use of hypnosis with analysis. Both these patients went easily into hypnosis, which enabled them to recall childhood incidents. The cathartic effect of this helped both patients. Sometimes, recalling forgotten childhood memories is not sufficient in itself. In these cases, it was.

In both cases I didn't say very much, except to question the patients about the dreams they told me and to put them into hypnosis, suggesting that they would remember the causes of their problems.

The first case is one which, although not typical, does illustrate many of the problems which can arise between parents and children. This patient, a man of 23, wanted to join the training course to become a practitioner. As always with trainees at The Psychotherapy Centre, he had to complete the appropriate amount of therapy first. Not only can this sort out the patient's problems, enabling him to become a competent practitioner, but the treatment itself is also a learning process.

This patient wasn't married, but he had a steady girlfriend with whom he got on well, having sex regularly. He was unaware that he had any emotional problems, but he admitted that both his parents were unable to express their feelings openly. He was an only child, which, he said, had no adverse effect as he believed his childhood was a happy one. He was intelligent, and had a degree in psychology. Prior to seeing me he had become interested in group therapy, taking a training course in biodynamic psychology, which he found unsatisfactory, and was sceptical about the efficacy of it, as after a year's study, which included participation in group therapy, he hadn't noticed any change in himself.

I agreed to take him on, saying I needed to see him at least three times a week. Later, he decided to come five times a week. He was paying for the therapy himself, which involved a considerable financial sacrifice.

In this account I've limited myself to minimum comments, reporting mainly what the patient said.

At his first session after the consultation he said:

'The consultation raised a lot of self-doubts. These lasted two weeks, then again over the last two days. I had a bad night last night, and an attack of diarrhoea this morning.' He remembered that, as a child, he was frightened of flushing the toilet. He also said he had spent two years decrying my form of treatment in favour of a humanistic approach. 'I didn't like you sitting behind the desk (at the consultation). I wanted to be pally. You didn't react to my manner.

'After my consultation with you I found I was better at standing up for myself. I said "No" to my flatmate. I felt funny afterwards. I felt anxious when I was about six years old. I once thought my mother said "FIRE!" from the bathroom. I smashed my way in. She was on the toilet. She slammed the door in my face.

'I remember once my parents embracing. I felt I couldn't go in. I stood outside for half an hour. I had a fear of going into my parents' bedroom. It was a prohibited place. I have memories of being really ill. Mother coming in. I changed places with father. Mother's nice warm bed.'

At the next session he said:

'I came away on Friday feeling good. I enjoyed it. Every time I look at you I feel you're bored. Mother used to undermine everything I did. I remember buying my first pair of jeans. My father rejected me.

'When I was 10 years old, I wanted to take a girl to the cinema. My parents refused to allow me to do so. Later I was embarrassed taking a girl out. I used to go out behind my parents' back.'

At the following session I tried hypnosis, which was sooner than I normally do, but I felt this patient was responding well to therapy.

'Shopping . . . in a pram or pushchair. Walking along . . . little teddy-bear. I'm in pram. Throwing teddy-bear about. She's telling me not to throw it about. See Mum's legs . . . bottom half . . . black dress. She's talking to someone . . . see her face . . . young and smiling. I'm nibbling teddy's ear . . . nibbling my Mum's ear. I feel happy . . . got teddy-bear. I see mother's breast . . . warm. Nice . . . hugging teddy-bear.

'Sitting in little seat at back of bike. Dad's driving. People pointing their fingers at me . . . wagging. Mum's laughing at Dad . . . or me? Their heads are together . . . kissing . . . Mum laughing at me . . . no-one as good as Dad . . . mocking.'

At the next session, in hypnosis:

'Playing ball with Daddy. He kicks the ball way up into the air. I think it's going to disappear. How can he kick it so far? Dad's the manager of the football team. I have to be there. People talking about Dad. Not nice. I pretend I'm not there. In the kitchen at home. Friends say they don't want me in football team. Mum and Dad will always be there.'

In the next session, in hypnosis, he recalled his first attempts at walking:

'I just manage to walk. Get to where Mummy is. Wrap my arms around her . . . frightening but good.

'Walking by myself . . . nobody to catch me . . . fall over . . . hurt my knee . . . I get up and fall down (he starts crying). Don't know where I'm going . . . few more paces . . . fall over . . . got to get up again . . . so difficult . . . fall over again. Not so bad now . . . getting used to it . . . know I can get up. (He smiles.) 'Wobble along . . . look forward to falling over again. Mother there . . . picks me up . . . asks me what I've been doing. I point to floor . . . falling over . . . not too bad . . . really frightening at beginning.'

The next time he came he said:

'I feel good after hypnosis. Pleasurable images of my mother. Unpleasant images of fingers being wagged at me. People angry.' In hypnosis:

'Walking with Mum in a crowd . . . she isn't there. People around . . . confused. I can only stand and look up . . . big people. People talking and shouting . . . Mum's always there . . . not now. Don't like this at all . . . Mum coming back . . . safe. Taking me to school . . . don't want to go. Holding someone's hand. Mum going and leaving me. I want to be at home. Mum going away over fields. Other children . . . strange . . . different coloured skin . . . wish Mum was black. Don't understand these people . . . warm at home . . . people not nice.

'Another school . . . older . . . Mum made me a blazer . . . no lapels . . . different. I'll have to tell Mum about this.

'Mum dressing in other room . . . can see her shadow . . . door open. Bloody hell! Dad's in there . . . taking her dress off.

'I run up steps "Mum! Mum! . . . boys bothering me" . . . "You have to stick up for yourself." Why doesn't she stick up for me? What's Daddy doing? I stepped on his pet budgie. He let me play with it. If Dad is angry . . . why doesn't he say so?

'Been naughty again . . . throwing milk bottles at cars. Mum says: "Wait till Daddy gets home!" He doesn't mind . . . he's more frightened of mother. He wants to play with my meccano set. Now he's really angry . . . funny, only because I'm asking questions, hits me. Bloody man, what's wrong with him? He's got it all wrong. I could blow up the Houses of Parliament and get away with it . . . but would get a beating if I put jam on the butter.

'Sunday lunch. Pleasant and warm . . . music . . . nice music . . . all happy. I don't want any roast beef . . . they get nasty . . . what's wrong with these bloody people?'

In the next session he told a dream:

'My girlfriend was with another man. She told me she was going on holiday with him, not me. I got so angry. I ranted and raved. She left the house. I attacked the man. He turned into a cardboard box. I jumped on it . . . smashed it to pieces.'

He said that jumping on the cardboard box was like jumping on his father's chest. He saw his girlfriend as his mother.

In hypnosis he said:

'There are faces shouting . . . like a football crowd. I run to be in the middle. Standing there alone . . . very small . . . whole world shouting and screaming. I started to stamp my feet. Stop shouting!

'Landlady downstairs shouting at me Mum. Mum tells me to get on with what I'm doing. She cries in corner. I want to go across to see what's wrong. Argument with grandparents. Uncle won't stop playing bloody piano. Nobody will tell me anything . . . whole family arguing. I'm going to get a hammer and smash that bloody piano. All the aggro goes above my head . . . I don't interfere . . . I sit in armchair and put my head in my arms.

'On holiday with Mum and Dad. I'm really shy. Someone taking picture. I don't like it . . . my Mum's legs.

'Strange man on the other side of street. He waves to me. I wave back. Mum tells me off. I won't wave at anybody or talk to them. Only trust Mum, I don't always trust Dad. Mum always says: "Wait till your father comes home!" Usually he's as nice as pie.

'Girl lives round the corner. Plays war games . . . dresses like a boy . . . confusing. Another girl, my cousin. Tries to kiss me. Doesn't seem right . . . push her off. In back of car . . . although I push her off, I like it.

'In same bedroom as Mum and Dad . . . their breathing is horrific. I'll have to tell Mum and Dad about it in the morning. I'm supposed to have an afternoon nap. I call Mum . . . not there. I call and call and call.'

In the following session, in hypnosis:

'Someone riding bike. I'm on back. Dad's riding . . . going to the park. Going too fast . . . got to get off.

'Standing holding someone's hand . . . grandmother. All in black. Tells me to stop doing things. Running down stairs.

'Playing in garden. Hear them talking about bringing friends through their part of the house. Two of them want to take their trousers down. I do too. In a park something really wrong. Quite excited. Mum says: 'What have you been doing?' I didn't tell her – she wouldn't like it. Things like that are not spoken about . . . not done.

'She says: "Stop playing with yourself!" I shouldn't say anything rude or naughty. It's fun . . . should do it. These things are always hushed up.

'In my bedroom . . . hear what they're talking about . . . they think I'm asleep. I hear what they're talking about . . . them and me. Wondering if I know facts of life. Why don't they ask me? Mum not sure. Dad knows. She says: "Jerry doesn't mind walking in front of me naked, but I wouldn't in front of him." '

At the next session he reported that he had been feeling quite different in the last few days. He realised that he'd a lot of aggression inside but had not been letting it out.

At one session he was ten minutes late. He said that the train had broken down. He had felt swamped by people around him. He said that it was like when his mother gave him too much to eat.

In hypnosis at another session he told me:

'Having dinner . . . friend coming. I ask: "Where do I put tomato skins?" I get shouted and bawled at. Asking silly questions. Asking and asking. Being ignored. Important to me . . . never come across the problem before. Dinner not a friendly place. Got to keep quiet. Being in a pram . . . should be . . . I'd much rather be pushed around in pram . . . sit in the pram and watch the world go by. Being pushed to write

'. . . pushed again . . . too much effort writing all them words . . . no power to say no.'

In another session, a week later, he told me in hypnosis:

'Plastic milk bottle . . . brown teat . . . just out of reach . . . can't get any milk out of it . . . nothing there . . . nothing coming out . . . straining. Pushed into my mouth . . . hard. Being taken away . . . going . . . I can relax . . . much better. Pan of hot boiling milk . . . I reach up and try and . . . take hold of handle. Pan comes out and covers me . . . hot . . . mother rushes over . . . takes sweater off . . . burning . . . bathes me in water . . . shoulder and arms . . . painful . . . can't get jumper off . . . hot . . . struggle.'

In his next session he recalled his first experiences at school:

'In room . . . see top of chairs . . . I'm wandering around . . . crashing into things . . . Mum puts my arms round her neck . . . carries me . . . feel someone's pulling me . . . at waist . . . I'm crying . . . don't want to go . . . hanging on for dear life . . . someone pulling and tugging . . . I'm hanging on . . . was cosy before . . . I'm gripping lapels . . . got me by trousers, pulling . . . my grip fails . . . I let go . . . bury my head in new shoulder . . . start thumping it . . . carrying me away . . . thumping . . . lots of people around . . . I cry . . . I get put down in another room. New woman . . . not the same . . . not the same warmth . . . trying to tell me to do things . . . classroom . . . people saying "that was you crying" . . . beginning to feel bigger and tougher . . . people bouncing off me . . . go back home to Mum at end of day . . . put up with this inconvenience.

'Pram . . . she's behind me pushing . . . get out of pram . . . start walking . . . such a difference . . . walk miles away.'

At another session he told me that he didn't communicate with his father.

'Only contact is with my mother. Father coming home in the evening after work. Lot of threats were not carried out. When I was 12 years old I was caught stealing. Had to go and face Dad. Mother screaming. He only said three or four words. I stole some records. Memory of Dad hitting me once.'

At another session he remembered, in hypnosis, his feelings towards his father, wanting to bite and chew him:

'Waving my arms around . . . reaching . . . I get picked up . . . carried . . . my arms round her neck . . . nice. Dad came along . . . puts his finger in my mouth . . . Mum puts me half over her shoulder . . pats me on the back . . . I start crying . . . Dad walks around . . . puts his finger in my mouth again . . . I bite it hard . . . makes me feel upset . . . I want to bite it off and chew it. Makes me feel sad he's getting too close . . . chop his finger off . . . cut it off . . . want to cut him up . . . he should stay away. Image of us getting changed in cubicle after swimming . . . his penis . . . easier to do it to his finger . . . so big . . . too big . . . can't do it . . . no way I can match that . . . anxiety goes now . . . back on Mum's shoulder . . . relaxing. Dad's still circling me . . . not so threatening.'

Another time in hypnosis:

'Choking sound . . . throaty . . . somebody vomiting – coughing . . . inside my chest . . . gargling noises . . . scream . . . can't come out . . . screaming . . . Mum's and Dad's faces . . . they cause scream to be inside me . . . they're not doing anything . . . shrug their shoulders . . . me in the middle . . . cold.

'They are taking a shelf off the wall . . . been there for years . . . I can't join in . . . sit in corner and watch . . . turning into anger.

'Mum and Dad holding my hand . . . taking me to hospital . . . stomach pains . . . really bad . . . stuck a pin in my stomach . . . to make my stomach hurt . . . they didn't know . . . stuck it right in navel. Doctor put on rubber gloves . . . inserted his finger into my anus . . . hurt . . . terrible. I stuck pin in to get attention and finish up in hospital without them and doctor sticking finger up my bum.

'Running along between them holding their hands . . . want to run ahead . . . fall over . . . cut my knees and hands . . . hurts so much . . . kept telling me to stop crying . . . the world beyond them is so frightening and painful.'

At another session he told me, in hypnosis:

'Dog I used to play with . . . black spotty dog. Got ill . . . went away for a long time . . . I asked where it was . . . "At the vet's." Finally told me it had been put down . . . they shouldn't keep things like that from me . . . why did they bother to tell me in the end? They let me down . . . Dad's idea.

'Wooden cot with bars . . . like play pen . . . bars across top of stairs . . . bars all over the place . . . can't get out of anything . . . all a plot . . . they don't trust me at all. Mustn't go in their room . . . can't get toys out . . . all a plot.

'Someone making a bed . . . Dad making a bed . . . throwing sheets in the air . . . I dislike going into their bedroom.

'Want to go to the toilet . . . good idea to do it on floor, they won't even know . . . do it on the floor . . . naughty . . . do it underneath their bed . . . they won't even know. I'll never get caught . . . really seems evil . . . just after they'd cleared everything up. They don't know, but I do. Serves them right for plotting against me.'

At another session he remembered in hypnosis his first feelings about sex and masturbation:

'Family party . . . Christmas? . . . all adults go out for drink in pub . . . children play games. This happened lots of times. Cousin a bit older than me . . . he wants to play rude games . . . wants people to take clothes off . . . too naughty . . . all girls giggle. They don't want to know . . . go and play somewhere else. Idea seems too shocking . . . once the thought was there it seemed OK. Barricaded doors and took our clothes off . . . so exciting . . . really exciting . . . naughtiest thing you could possibly do.

'In garage with another friend . . . took our trousers down . . . locked his sister out . . . she wanted to get in . . . made it all the more exciting . . . we masturbated. His sister manages to get box to stand on . . . looks through window . . . "I can see you!"

'My other friend had lots of sisters . . . all a bit younger . . . going round to his house . . . bath time . . . his older sister just had a bath. She came into the room . . . she sat down opposite. Took her towel off and laughed. Seemed exciting but it was naughty. Not supposed to do that . . . his parents must have thought it funny, I kept going round at 7 o'clock on Thursdays.

'In woods with everybody . . . a whole crowd . . . my turn . . . didn't know what I was doing . . . more exciting thinking about it . . . nothing really happened . . . lying on ground behind big tree . . . all my friends shouting . . . didn't know what to do. Always more exciting to think about it than doing it . . . crowd egging me on.

'First time I went into room to do it I fumbled . . . tried to get Durex out . . . "What are you doing?" . . . I dropped everything . . . didn't try much after that . . . earlier attempts pathetic.

Mum telling me off . . . shouting at me. "Don't do that!" Playing with yourself and nose-picking in same category. Just did it when they were not around . . . they always seemed to be around. My bedroom next to the lounge . . . didn't stop me . . . had to do it quietly.'

Another time he told me in hypnosis about further sexual feelings:

'Staying with cousin . . . spiteful . . . dominated me . . . also friendly and pally . . . he seemed to know about everything . . . had elder sister. He used to tell me stories . . . having to sleep with his sister . . . hard to believe . . . used to tell my about kissing girls. He'd done so much more than me . . . so much fun. Images of me Mum . . . I wasn't allowed to think about things he'd done . . . I feel too guilty. See cousin's face . . . see Mum's face . . . having thoughts about Ann . . . would be the same as thoughts about mother.'

At the following session he continued with his sexual thoughts about his mother, going into fantasy:

'Standing . . . Mum's doing shopping . . . following her . . . boring. . . she's turned into . . . she's naked . . . lying on bed naked. I'm lying on top of her . . . making love . . . feels stiff. Can't do anything . . . as if she was in lots of different poses . . . as if everything inside me stopping me enjoying it. Pleasant thoughts . . . so painful' (he starts to cough and splutter) '. . . it's too much. I can't do it . . . every time I see her body it becomes unpleasant. Images of her poses . . . I can't do anything . . . I feel paralysed . . . I just can't let go . . .

165

image is too powerful . . . waked unpleasant physical reaction. Physically attractive yet causes revulsion . . . image of father behind me . . . checking I don't get too close. I want to be in union . . . black figure behind me . . . power of his figure being there.'

Out of hypnosis he told me he felt shaky, as if he'd vomited. He felt he'd cleared something out.

At another session he had a fantasy of confronting his father. This showed his enormous mental struggle with his father. Patients often have fantasies in hypnosis, and this is an example.

'I feel people are watching me . . . a whole gallery . . . as I perform. They are all whispering . . . I can't hear. I want to run and hide. Aunts and uncles, relations and parents. What's going to become of me? Like a boxing match. I've got a massive boxing glove on . . . clout him out of the way . . . keeps on coming one after another . . . fighting back . . . audience loving it. It's a struggle . . . cheers and shouts . . . who's going to win? I step into the ring again . . . referee tells them to go into their corners . . . father around somewhere . . . in the ring . . . wait his turn . . . one huge battle . . . massive . . . have audience on their feet . . . I don't know if I'm a contestant or the referee. All my strength to fight mammoth boxer . . . bide my time. Audience egging me on . . . on my side . . . bell's gone . . . standing in corner . . . can't come out.' (At this point he starts crying.) 'People in my corner pushing . . . can't let them down. Too frightening . . . I take a knife out with me . . . I need the advantage . . . I want to rush and slash him . . . not meet him face to face. I walk into the ring with big gun and blast it . . . weapon so big that he can't get into the ring. Like a huge cannon. I want to take one step forward and slap him round the face . . . bastard . . . I feel I want to explode.' (At this point his fantasy stopped.)

'My father once asked me to go out and do some shopping. It was a cold Saturday night. I stood and stared at him. I didn't want to go. I went in the end. I shouldn't let him win.'

At his next session he spoke of his father.

'As a child I could never believe that I was wanted around. I didn't trust my parents. I didn't trust my father or his intentions. I wish my father was dead.' (Pause.) 'I don't believe I wanted to say that.'

At another session he remembered another incident from childhood:

'I'm on a pond with Dad. He gets angry and shouts at me. I don't like it when he shouts. If Mum was here he wouldn't shout. I'm being continually told off.'

At another session:

'I'm cold . . . wrapped up in winter clothes . . . being pushed in a chair . . . got my hat on . . . Mum pushing me . . . leans over and makes sure I'm warm . . . she does top button up.

'Mum and Dad together . . . he cuts me off from having Mum. They're kidding for ages and ages . . . can only see them through the glass . . . can't go into the room . . . bedroom. I'm in the other room. I don't belong there . . . separate room.

'I'm naked . . . I don't know what to do . . . he's standing there . . . I can't do anything . . . all because of him watching.'

At another session he remembered one of his first sexual experiences with girls:

'Playing a game with my cousins. Trying to put our hands up our cousins' dresses . . . one of them tells my Mum. Doing naughty things and telling lies. Tried to

167

force dirt into baby's mouth.'

At the next session he automatically went into hypnosis without any prompting on my part. Prior to this he told me a dream regarding his mother which frightened him:

'I find this dream frightening . . . wanting my mother sexually . . . I feel the hole is pulling me or I'm pulling myself in. Seemed so compelling . . . if I go inside it's going to be black nothing. Restricts all my movements . . . hurts . . . makes me feel tight . . . I want to shrug it off. It's black and soft . . . like being pushed along . . . it oozed.

'I feel I've been inside, back inside my mother . . . every inch of the way was a struggle. Just for a moment at the end I let go. Struggle stopped . . . being held. Then I was back here. It was like being held in the womb. Everything is brighter now.'

At the following session he told me a dream where he was fighting people off, especially one man who turned into a book. He then ripped the pages out, one by one.

'It's too painful a thought . . . destroying my father . . . actually killing him. Images of my father . . . hanging in front of me . . . cut to pieces.'

At the following session he told me that he had felt very guilty about what he had said the previous session about killing his father. In hypnosis he recounted his impressions about his parents and sex:

'They're together in the kitchen . . . always together. They want to move my bed from their bedroom into another room. Putting me outside . . . discarded . . . throw me away . . . why can't I stay there? . . . throwing me out. Partition between my bedroom and theirs . . . hardly worth having one. They're getting ready to undress . . . can hear it all . . . as if I wasn't there . . . I wasn't supposed to be there. They moved me from there to another room . . . hardboard walls . . . no privacy . . . they thought I couldn't hear. I didn't want to be there . . . paper-thin walls . . . horrible . . . me and them. Not supposed to be here . . . not supposed to hear them. Could hear my Mum getting undressed . . . images . . . I had to dismiss them . . . I wasn't supposed to be there. Spend my life trying not to be there . . . but I am there. As if people can hear my thoughts . . . people can hear what I'm thinking. Everything in me is public . . . felt guilty . . . everybody knows what I'm thinking. Try not to think . . . paper-thin walls . . . I feel guilty so I'll try and be nice. Parents made love and I could hear it. Clear as a bell . . . no way it could have been any different. That's the way it was . . . some part of me that's private. Bloody cardboard walls . . . living in a glass-house . . . bloody glass-house . . . everybody looking in . . . no corners to hide in. Can only run to my Mum . . . secure . . . absolutely naked . . . like walking around with an erection . . . everyone can see. Kill my father . . . only way to resolve it . . . me and Mum. That thought feels so public . . . paper-thin between me and the world . . . I feel weak . . . given a knife I couldn't stab him.'

The following session he told me a dream:

'I'm making love to a woman . . . she alternates between my mother and my girlfriend. I'm trying to get her to get her clothes off. "What will your father think?" I'm undoing her buttons. She lies naked in front of me. Changes into my girlfriend.'

In hypnosis he remembered feeling guilty about being naughty:

'I'm standing on the opposite side of the room . . . very stiff . . . must have done something wrong . . . lots of things . . . like rolling milk bottles in front of cars . . . throwing dirt in pram.'

Then he remembered an incident about sexual exploration.

'Going up to the top of the hill . . . taking our trousers off . . . frightened that mother might know.'

At another session he recalled his ambivalent feelings towards his father.

'How can I get rid of my father if he is such a source of security? . . . Why can't they both go? . . . they come again . . . appear again . . . they won't go . . . always following me around . . . I need to get close to them . . . especially my mother.'

He remembered that he felt that as a child his parents did not attach much importance to what happened outside the house as far as their child was concerned.

'The police caught me for stealing . . . parents hardly said anything. Mother telling me what I did outside home and school was my own affair. Rules of the house . . . for their benefit. What the neighbours think . . . arguments would flare . . . what does it matter?'

At another session he remembered, in hypnosis, his ambivalent feelings about his feminine feelings and his death wishes towards his parents:

'Mother making me put on dresses . . . try them out for my cousins . . . I don't want to . . . sissy . . . eventually put them on . . . get to like it after a bit. I ask her if she has any more dresses to put on.

'Crying and crying in bed . . . thoughts of Mum and Dad dying . . . horrible . . . I used to cry and cry.'

This patient told me another fantasy in hypnosis:

'They're still there together . . . on the settee . . . as if they were . . . imagination . . . goes wild. Naked in front of me . . . me or my father?' (he laughs) 'they've gone . . . just me on the settee . . . naked . . . really funny. She's just lying down beside me . . . masturbating me all the time. Father back again . . . OK so long as I can have my turn again. "Your go now" . . . so polite to each other.'

He was getting disturbed by his feelings towards his mother. At the next session he confused reality with fantasy. In hypnosis he told me:

'Someone pulling their pants down . . . I can hear her undressing in the bedroom next to mine . . . just hearing it conjures up images. I can't avoid hearing it . . . father taking his trousers off. There to tempt me . . . covering and uncovering. Thoughts of entering her from behind' (he laughs) '. . . I don't want it to happen' (laughs) '. . . copulation incredible' (laughs) 'like masturbation. This bum there' (laughs) 'just there . . . as if I'm holding her by the scruff of the neck . . . too vicious . . . thrusting . . . nasty vicious. Almost as if she's tempting me to do it . . . taking her underwear off' (laughing) 'like masturbating . . . using someone to masturbate into . . . abuse . . . fucking all the time. Only want to make contact with my penis . . . don't want rest of my body to touch.'

Some parents are insensitive about what their children can hear and understand. This patient's parents were like that:

'In my bedroom . . . could hear Mum and Dad talking in next room. I didn't want to hear that . . . she can't be totally truthful . . . stupid thing to say . . . he must know I can hear him . . . Mother being naked in front of father. Undressing next door as if she was undressing in front of me . . . seducing me.'

At another session he told me:

'Dad bursts into tears . . . cries . . . I didn't realise

171

why . . . he sulked . . . I cried also . . . his father taken to hospital and was dying. I'd not seen father cry before . . . mother also went upstairs and cried. Want to kill father and also cry with him.

'Massive great penis . . . get confused . . . saw his penis in the bath . . . his is so big and mine so small.'

The patient's annoyance with his father was a recurring theme. In hypnosis he said:

'I can see him . . . he's around again . . . becoming a fucking pain . . . going to my cousin's . . . he tells my aunt I could stay . . . then tells me that I couldn't . . . saying one thing and then another.

' "You have to go down to the shops – don't argue!" I could have murdered him . . . I was just staring at him.

'I can't do anything . . . leave me alone! Bugger off!'

In one session he told me a dream where he felt that his mother wanted to seduce him:

'In a cinema . . . I sat at the back and waited for the show to start. Girl next to me – dressed like a tart . . . trying to attract my attention. "You can have me if you want." She leant across and grabbed my penis. "Come on, we'll do it now." I wanted to apologise to my girlfriend . . . never found her . . . felt guilty.'

Then in hypnosis he continued:

'Girl in my dream . . . teasing me again . . . rolling about in front of me naked . . . keeps on teasing me . . . keeps asking me to come over . . . OK if she's at a distance . . . just a disguise . . . as long as it stays that way . . . becomes more and more like my mother . . . just lying there. I'm drawn into it . . . can't refuse . . . can't do it. Keeps on exposing herself . . . my mother there all the time . . . I'm pretending it's not her . . . I want to climb on top.'

At this point in the therapy, sex was very prominent in his thoughts. At one session, in hypnosis, he told me:

'In a car . . . powerful thing . . . like an erection . . . power thing . . . throbbing thing. Getting up in the mornings with and without erections. Something between my legs . . . powerful throbbing . . . vulnerable . . . feels good.

'Masturbating . . . I shouldn't be doing it . . . paper-thin walls . . . parents next door . . . masturbate every night. Tried to resist it but couldn't . . . throbbing too nice. It was good, it was bad, it was good. Oh, Christ! Every fucking night . . . felt good. Didn't deter me . . . going to maximum limit of noise . . . they must hear me . . . every bloody night. Father having bath once . . . saw his penis . . . I walked straight in . . . he tried to hide himself . . . his prick was completely different.'

The patient's feelings towards his mother were becoming more apparent, which disturbed him. In hypnosis he told me:

'Mother laughing and tossing her head back . . . want to take all her clothes off . . . lie down and screw daylights out of her. Each piece of clothing off . . . part her legs . . . throbbing prick . . . put inside her cunt. That's what I want to do . . . these thoughts are so vulnerable they are going to collapse . . . that's what I want to do . . . gets frightening . . . it's just going to go. It's going to be cut off . . . so vulnerable . . . as if my father is going to come along with bowling balls and go "crash!"'

At the next session he continued in much the same vein:

'Tremendous arguments going on . . . father shouting. I was making paper plane . . . throwing it across the room . . . he got angry with me . . . shouted . . . hit me . . . my head hit mantelpiece . . . sent me upstairs . . . I was terrified. He's too powerful . . . could hit me across the room. I want to rape my mother . . . fuck everyone else around me . . . you, my father, everyone. Going to rape with this fucking great cock of mine. Getting muddled . . . you or my father I'm scared of? He's going to come round and snap it off. See who's going to give in first . . . I've got this fucking great erection and I'm going to use it.'

His feelings towards his mother were getting stronger and stronger all the time, which led to him having a sense of guilt about them. In hypnosis, he told me:

'Everything turning into fucking all the time. I don't trust it any more. Scenes of rape and fucking . . . won't go away . . . all I want to do is screw and rape my mother . . . image of her lying there . . . penetration and rape. Dad's going to come along with a bloody great axe . . . chop my bollocks off.'

Some sessions later he was still talking about his father's penis, comparing it with his own:

'Father's always got this big cock . . . I couldn't possibly satisfy Mum with this little thing. He's just standing there . . . huge prick . . . "You can never match this" is what he's saying.'

At school he also felt he had to compare his penis with those of the other boys.

'I keep seeing two cocks . . . keep seeing my father. Embarrassed in showers with small prick . . . others had huge hairy cocks . . . little tiny white thing . . . so ashamed of it.'

At another session he told me in hypnosis:

'I was going to a fancy dress party . . . as a girl . . . mother wouldn't let me change at home . . . had to go to a friend's.'

He still had conflicts about his feelings and his competition with his father.

'I can't bite the hand that feeds me. My nickname used to be Tubby . . . used to have tits when I was fat . . . big tits and tiny cock.'

He eventually got round to tackling his parents and was quite surprised by the result. He told me (not in hypnosis):

'I told my parents over the weekend some of the things on my mind . . . very successful. I was fascinated to hear their side of the story. I was a bit frightened . . . started with my mother. Father realised that he had to come into it. I told him I resented and hated him. He said he understood. I was amazed. He told me of a period when I wouldn't go to sleep without someone holding my hand. For an hour before I went to sleep. This went on for weeks. Father said he regretted many things he'd done. He told me I had once got lost in a crowd. He was very pleased to find me but got annoyed and shouted at me.

'I told him that I didn't understand some of their rules. How he had interfered. They told me that when I was 14 years old I became detached and distant. My mother got worried. I would often lose things. I haven't lost anything for ages then yesterday I lost my keys. Mother also told me she found it difficult to show affection.'

From this point the patient made great strides in his therapy, eventually getting married and starting a family. He was co-operative throughout his treatment, which made my task easy and his recovery speedy and successful.

The second case concerns a girl of 26 who came to

see me for emotional problems. She said that she didn't 'fit in', suffering from severe depression, but was too cowardly to commit suicide. She was also afraid of men, not being able to form a normal sexual relationship. She came from Australia, and had been away from home for two years. Her parents wanted her to return, which made her feel guilty about staying away. Her father was a stubborn, domineering man, who often got drunk, which made him violent. On one occasion, she told me, he broke her mother's jaw. She also told me that she had been an unwanted pregnancy and had been conceived out of wedlock. In addition, her father had wanted a boy, not a girl.

I shall describe the salient events in the treatment of the patient in the sequence in which they occurred. I have made few comments, leaving you to reach your own conclusions.

The patient had a very traumatic childhood, and I doubt if she would have made much progress in treatment without hypnosis being used. With two or three exceptions, hypnosis was used on every visit. In hypnosis, the patient always regressed to early childhood or babyhood. Apart from helping her to examine her dreams and to go into hypnosis, I kept silent. The cathartic effect of hypnosis on this patient benefitted her with the minimum of interference.

As usual with new patients, I had to decide whether hypnosis was suitable and, if so, how soon to use it. I usually postpone using hypnosis, especially if the patient lays great store on its restorative powers. This time I decided to try hypnosis on her second visit and she appeared to go into it easily. Soon she was talking in hypnosis.

'My parents hate me. They always say they love me,

but I don't believe them. I was an accident to start with. It shouldn't have happened. My father thrashed me severely when I was six years old. I forgot to come home for lunch. He came to fetch me. He took off my pants and belted me. My parents were always fighting, usually over me.'

On her next visit, in hypnosis:

'There's a brick wall. My father's throwing something or someone at the wall.' (It was very painful for her to remember this.) 'My mother's screaming and screaming. I'm really scared. I'm very small. I don't think anything is broken. My mother is yelling and crying.

'There was something I wouldn't eat. There was fighting at every meal. I was forced to eat until I was sick. I used to have to go to bed early, while other children were playing till seven o'clock. I hated father for that.'

In the following session she said she was stunned at what she had said the previous time, and rejected it. She told me she had to wear leg irons until she was seven years old because of weak bones. She added that she resented people having pity on her.

She told me a dream in which she was being raped. 'It was really horrible.' It made her feel sick to think about it. In hypnosis:

'I was by myself, playing with a tea set. The man from downstairs came in. He took my dress off. I thought he was playing a game. Then he took off my vest and pants. He felt me all over. I was scared. He was rubbing his hands up and down me. Then he rubbed his penis over me. I was two or three years old.'

I then noticed that she began to have dreams which related directly to incidents which she was remembering in hypnosis. She dreamt once of 'wormy things' burrowing into her skin. In hypnosis:

'I used to go shopping with my mother. It was very boring. Once she beat me because I'd taken something shiny. It was bad to steal. A policeman would come and take me to jail. I couldn't understand what it was all about.'

Her father had constantly told her that she should have been a boy. So she became a tomboy, but her mother did not like her playing with boys. Why could she not be like other girls?

In one dream she saw herself in a pre-natal position, inside a big shell or seed. In the morning she could not wake up and when she did she felt as if she was miles away, and did not want to have anything to do with her flatmates.

She then had a dream of her parents wanting to kill her, and her dog being killed.

In another dream a policeman with a big stick broke into her flat.

In hypnosis:

'There was a stray dog. My father had a rifle. He shot it. Twice. I was terrified. He took it to the back garden and buried it. "Don't you ever tell your mother!"

'My father had a blue pot to help me go to the toilet. After every meal I had to sit on it, until I had done something. I was scared to death. He held me and I yelled. I was so scared I couldn't do anything. Sometimes I was sick.

'My parents were talking in bed. My father wanted to send me away to a children's home. I was an accident anyway. They had a big argument about it. Afterwards they had sex.'

She dreamt of taking an overdose of tablets. She was

on a stretcher with people in white standing around her. She also dreamt of going into hospital and when she came out her car had gone.

In hypnosis:

'I was outside, playing in the garden with the little boy from next door. His mother took our clothes off and we kicked around in the sunshine. I could see that our bodies were really different. I wondered why. I didn't have the thing boys had. There was something wrong with me. I didn't have a penis. We played with one another. My mother came over and yelled: "THAT'S DIRTY! DON'T TOUCH OTHER PEOPLE!" She hit us both. I couldn't understand why she smacked us. I started to cry. Why was I different? She never answered my questions.'

At another visit, in hypnosis:

'I was playing outside on my rug. My father was looking after me. I went to the toilet. I was uncomfortable. I wanted my nappy changed. I started to cry, and began pulling faeces out of my nappy and putting them all over the rug. My father saw this and bellowed: "STOP IT!" I stood up and he pushed me hard against a wall and hurt my head. My mother was screaming: "STOP IT!" '

Her father repeatedly told her that he wished she had been a boy. She could not work out why she was different from little boys. Why could she not play with the little boy's penis?

She had another dream of being raped. She was terrified. In the next session, in hypnosis:

'My father picked me up and put me in my cot. We were alone in the flat. I didn't like him coming near me. He went out and came back without any clothes on. He was drinking from a bottle. I started crying and he got angry. He picked me up and put me on the bed. He jumped on top of me. He took my nappy and singlet off and started rubbing his body all over me. His penis was all wet. I kept screaming but he wouldn't stop.'

In the next session, in hypnosis:

'The mosquito netting fell down over me. My father came in. He put his big hand over me. I tried to . . . I couldn't breathe. I started screaming. He was always rough. He was bathing me. His hands were all over me and tickled. I hated being tickled between the legs. He pushed my face down under the water. Did he want to drown me? I spluttered and gasped. "Be quiet. Little boys wouldn't do that." '

She had a dream in which she was very small and sitting on the floor. There was a big rat running up and down. She wanted cats to chase it away. In hypnosis:

'There was a big grey thing, a mouse or a rat, racing across the room. It ran over my legs. My mother became hysterical. My father caught the mouse and knocked it out. He picked it up by the tail and dangled it in front of my nose. My mother was frightened of mice and father hated cats.'

In the following session, in hypnosis:

'My father was screaming at my mother. So was my grandmother. They wanted her to go away and take me. My mother was crying. My father rushed in and grabbed me by the arms and threw me to my mother. "GET OUT!" They were shouting obscene words. My father almost hit her with a bottle. He smashed it on the table and held the jagged end. My mother took some clothes and we went next door.'

In the same session, in hypnosis:

'My father was running around with no clothes on. He picked me up and started throwing me up into the air. The woman from downstairs came up with a bottle. They finished it and then took all my clothes off, including my nappy. They were both laughing. I wet the carpet. My father screamed at me and struck me on the legs. I was crying. "She's got to learn not to. The sooner she goes the better." The woman sat down next to me and started tickling me. I was screaming. My father started swinging me up and down. Then they went into the bedroom. I heard hysterical laughter. Then it was quiet. My father came out wearing nothing. He picked me up and put me on the bed. He went out and had a drink. He came back and started to jump on me. He rubbed me up and down his stomach and between his legs. Then he rubbed his penis up and down my back.'

On another visit, in hypnosis:

'The lady downstairs often used to look after me. She drank a lot. Once I was in my cot on her bed. She came in smelling of alcohol. She was laughing. She didn't have any clothes on. I was scared. She took my clothes off and rubbed her hands all over me. My father was also there, in his underwear. I was screaming. He was grinning at me.'

Her father had wanted a boy. She could not get this thought out of her head. He wanted to get rid of her.

She told me a dream she had of a baby with a big penis. In hypnosis:

'I was in a dark room. It was late. My mother and father had gone out. My grandmother was there listening to the radio. A man arrived. She brought him in and put the light on. He smelled of alcohol and was laughing. They went out and switched the light off. Then he came back in. He was drunk and making strange noises. I was afraid and started to cry. He picked me up and started to play with me. He had big thick fingers. He put his hands all over me, even down to the lower regions. I was crying and screaming. He put his face close to mine: "sh . . . sh . . ." He took off his pants and lay down on the bed. He put my hand on his penis. Then he rubbed it up and down and rolled over me.'

At the next session she related a dream about having stabbed someone to death. There were big bloody gashes. She was holding a pair of scissors.

In hypnosis:

'I was awake in my cot in a darkened room. I could see a shadow. I was scared and started to cry. A man took me out of my cot and put me on the bed. He put his hands down on my face. They were very big. One hand was over my mouth. I couldn't breathe. I couldn't make any noise. He started taking my nappy off. Then the light went on and my father and mother came into the room. They were screaming and yelling. My father grabbed a knife or a pair of scissors. He slashed the other man on the arm. He fell to the floor. My mother was screaming. She grabbed me. She was hysterical. There was blood all over the place.'

In the following session she remembered a friend who had shot herself. There were pools of blood. She also said that she had been vomiting all that morning for no apparent reason. She kept on thinking of dead bodies.

She had dreamt that she was trying to get a driver's licence. She couldn't, and gave up.

In hypnosis:

'I was downstairs, on a rug on the floor. Hands were looking after me. I kept reaching up for long dark hair. My mother came down. She took her clothes off. They were laughing, and running up and down playing "catch me". Then they got into bed. I fell asleep. I woke up hungry. My mother fed me. The other woman started playing with me. I hated her.'

In the next session she said that she had been disturbed by her mother's lesbian tendencies. She also resented her mother.

At another session she told me that she'd dreamt of her younger brother cutting one of his fingers off. Also a dream of a woman grabbing pens and pencils out of her hand, which made her furious.

In hypnosis:

'My mother let me down. She resented me as much as my father did. She couldn't go out dancing or play tennis. She was always looking for someone to look after me. I was often left in the cot. It used to get dark and I was hungry. I felt I was a burden to her.'

In the next session, in hypnosis:

'My mother was holding me. I had nothing on. My father was there. He said something about extra skin round my sexual area. He was looking at my legs and laughing. My mother was asking: "What shall we do about these?" My father said: "It costs money. We can't afford medical expense." Someone told them to have my legs seen to straight away or I wouldn't walk properly. There were special irons and boots that could straighten my feet. When I got my irons, my father used to laugh at me. He made a spectacle of me. I kept on falling over.'

At another session she related a dream in which she woke up covered in blood then got up and wiped it off with a tissue.

In hypnosis:

'There were people in white standing round me.

Something to do with my legs and feet. My mother went away. Someone in white picked me up. I could feel cold hands. I screamed. Different hands were feeling my legs and feet. They were not my mother's. My mother came back and took me home. It didn't last. I was taken back to the people in white. They were doing something to my legs. My mother wasn't there. She didn't come back for ages and I cried. Someone took me outside. The sun was warm. I was alone. Then my mother came and took me home. This seemed to happen many times. I always screamed when my mother put me down. I'd scream till I fell asleep. I was always afraid that they would take me away again.'

In the following session, in hypnosis:

'My father was in the lounge with a woman. It wasn't my mother. She had blonde hair. They were on the couch together, laughing. A man came in yelling and screaming. He was shouting about his wife and my father. "Wait until I tell your wife!" My father was furious. He started to yell and scream. The noise was terrifying. My father stabbed the man in the shoulder with a knife. Blood was running down his arm and dripping onto the floor. My father was in a violent rage and belting into the other man. His wife was screaming: "He's killing him! He's killing him!" The man left, saying: "I'll get you!" My father was mopping up. He told me: "Stop crying!" and to the other woman: "Shut up or you'll get some of it too!" He got a pillow and stuck a knife into it, and slashed it all up.

'The other man came back. His big cold hands were all over me. He put a cushion on my face. I couldn't breathe. My father came in with a knife. He stabbed him in the arm again and he fell down. There was blood on the floor. My father picked him up and dragged him out.

'My father was saying that I was too much of a burden. I would have to be sent away.

'I had to go into hospital at different times. My father was telling the neighbours how much I was costing in medical expenses. He was drinking and talking about money. He grabbed my mother and pushed her off the chair. She abused him. He picked up a table knife and slashed her across the arm. He was white with fury. My mother was horrified. Her arm was bleeding. My father was very violent. He would hurt anybody.'

At the next session, in hypnosis:

'My father was standing by the bed. My mother was holding me up for him. He'd been drinking. "Why couldn't it have been a boy? I would never have married you if I'd known you were going to have a girl." He didn't like me at all. What were they going to call me? They hadn't thought of girls' names. My father picked me up. He had big cold hands. I screamed. I was cold after being with my mother.

"What's wrong with her legs?"

"There's a weakness in the bones. They'll have to be strapped until they're stronger."

"Why couldn't you produce a healthy child?"

My mother was crying. A nurse took me away. I was screaming.'

In the next session she remembered playing with some boys. She thought she would be getting a penis. Why was she different? She thought she was going to grow one. She had an extra piece of skin over her clitoris. She then made a Freudian slip. She said: 'When I was *not* a girl.'

In the next session, in hypnosis:

'I was in the bath. My mother was sponging me. She

was talking about me. My father said I should have been a boy. He put his hand down and "made a penis" with his thumb. "She should have one of these. We don't want any more children. It's too expensive."'

That was her last session. She had to return home to Australia. She had attended forty-nine sessions over eight months, coming twice a week.

After the first two or three sessions she started getting worse rather than better, which often happens with patients before they begin to show signs of recovery. She became depressed and homesick. She also yelled in her sleep, much to the annoyance of her room-mate.

After eight sessions she felt the first signs of improvement. She began to feel confident and people were complimenting her on her changed behaviour. This embarrassed her. She also felt guilty about her aggressive feelings towards her mother which were coming out. She complained of pains in her stomach.

In the ninth week of treatment she said she was feeling better and sleeping well. She was more relaxed and was beginning to express her anger. She found that she could stand up to the headmaster of the school where she taught.

After thirty sessions she reported having met an old girl-friend who remarked how calm she had become. She had also spoken to her parents by telephone and had felt much more at ease. Her landlord had also remarked how she did not 'fly off the handle' quite so much.

She started losing her tomboy looks. She began taking an interest in her appearance and, at 26 years of age, was using make-up for the first time in her life; she had to ask one of her flat-mates how to put it on. She tried sex with a man, but still could not enjoy it. She felt he was using her and she couldn't trust him. She said she was afraid of becoming 'over-confident'.

Had she been able to complete treatment I believe she would have recovered completely.

In both of these cases, the patients went deeply into hypnosis, which enabled them to regress to childhood. In the last case, the patient was able to regress to a very early stage in her life. I doubt whether these recollections would have surfaced so vividly, if at all, had hypnosis not been used. Both patients may have benefitted or recovered from their problems without the use of hypnosis, but it would have been a much lengthier course of treatment. Provided patients respond well to hypnosis, therapy can be accelerated enormously. In treating emotional disorders, the therapy must suit the patient, not the other way round. Too many practitioners try to impose their treatment onto the patient, rather than supplying the correct therapy. In psychotherapy it's important to remember that patients are individuals and require individual attention. The therapy must be tailored to the patient's requirements, even if he is not appreciative of the fact at the time. A patient may have pre-conceived ideas about treatment and demand hypnosis, but it may not be suitable in his particular case. In these two cases hypnosis was appropriate.

Further reading

Robert Ardrey	**African Genesis**	*Fontana*
Robert Ardrey	**The Territorial Imperative**	*Fontana*
Robert Ardrey	**The Social Contract**	*Fontana*
R K Brian	**The Psychocats**	*The Psychotherapy Centre*
R K Brian	**The Laius Complex**	*The Psychotherapy Centre*
R K Brian	**Choosing A Psychotherapist**	*The Psychotherapy Centre*
R K Brian	**King Lear; Rejection**	*The Psychotherapy Centre*
R K Brian	**Why Be Psycho-Analysed Before Becoming A Psychotherapist?**	*The Psychotherapy Centre*
C O Carter	**Human Heredity**	*Pelican*
Robert Eagle	**Alternative Medicine**	*Futura*
Sir Keith Joseph	**The Cycle Of Deprivation**	*The Psychotherapy Centre*
Richard E Leakey and Roger Lewin	**Origins**	*Macdonald & Jane's*
Konrad Lorenz	**On Aggression**	*Methuen*
Desmond Morris	**The Naked Ape**	*Corgi*
A Stuart Mason	**Health And Hormones**	*Pelican*
Ian Oswald	**Sleep**	*Pelican*
Piers Paul Read	**Alive**	*Pan*
R D Rosen	**Psychobabble**	*Wildwood House*
Anthony Smith	**The Body**	*Pelican*
John Sparks	**The Sexual Connection**	*Sphere*
Anthony Storr	**Human Aggression**	*Pelican*
Anthony Storr	**Sexual Deviation**	*Pelican*
Lyall Watson	**Supernature**	*Coronet*

INDEX

abortion, 102, 148
abreaction, 24
absent parents, 43, 50, 51, 52, 54, 59, 60, 73
accidents, 71, 94
acne, 63
adoption, 40
addiction, 98
advice, 99
aggression, 9, 12, 14, 19, 49, 50, 53, 56, 67–74, 88, 94, 96, 100, 114, 131, 132, 143, 159, 160, 186, 188
alcohol, 30, 52, 54, 55, 58, 63, 80, 102, 127, 176, 181, 185
anaesthesia, 22
anal wishes, 37
anger, 66, 69–71, 73, 82, 84, 89, 112, 127, 138, 144, 157, 158, 163, 180, 186
anorexia, 32
anus, 41
anxiety, 30, 51, 53, 56, 60, 64, 131, 136, 151
apathy, 102, 129
arguing, 138, 170
asthma, 100
attention-getting, 33
authority-figures, 46
avoidance of marriage, 48
avoidance of men, 33–4
avoidance of women, 47

babies, 20, 26, 27, 28, 29, 30, 36, 37, 38, 76, 107, 148
back pain, 138
bad temper, 58, 71, 148
battered children, 45, 175–87
beards, 46, 49, 70
bed-wetting, 37

behaviour therapy, 147
birth, 9, 20, 22–9, 40, 41, 78, 83, 91
biting, 35, 36, 103, 162
blame, 134, 140, 152
blisters, 141
blue films, 61, 66
blushing, 63, 137
boarding schools, 38
bottles, 35
breast-feeding, 30, 35
breasts, 30, 35, 42, 43, 46, 49
British Hypnotherapy Association, 112
brothers, 21, 42, 44, 45, 47, 54, 59, 78, 81, 107, 183
bullying, 56, 69, 131, 134

cannibalism, 34–6
cars, 42, 71, 173
castration fear, 41, 42, 43, 56, 57, 60, 174
cat phobia, 26, 107–10, 141
catharsis, 154, 176
causes, 97–111, 154
censor, 91
chair, 44, 122
children, 13, 15, 20, 21, 27, 30, 32, 36, 38, 40, 41, 43, 44, 46, 48, 49, 50, 57, 59, 60, 63, 69, 73, 74, 75, 76, 77, 78, 82, 83, 84, 86, 87, 88, 89, 90, 104, 106, 129, 130, 133, 134, 139–44, 146, 154–86
cleanliness, 37
climax, 62
colds, 104
commuting, 43
competing, 59, 75, 76, 175
complaining, 62
compulsions, 33

conception, 40, 49, 90
confidence, 56, 58, 59, 85, 127, 131, 151, 152, 186
confidentiality, 129, 137
conformity, 87
confrontation, 139–44, 166, 175
conscious mind, 18, 91–4
constipation, 37, 60
consultation, 100, 102, 107, 110, 111, 114–22, 126–8, 129–34, 137, 155, 176
contradictory statements, 84, 172
couch, 44, 122
counter-transference, 118, 120
couples, 134–8
criticism, 74, 85, 140, 167
cunnilingus, 64

daughters, 22, 43, 45, 46, 48, 76, 77, 83, 88, 89, 129, 130, 131, 175–87
death, 22, 98, 106
defecation, 36–8, 60
déjà-vu, 25
dependency, 20, 98, 129, 130, 131, 138, 140, 152
depression, 102, 104, 122, 131, 132, 176
dermatitis, 105
destructiveness, 29, 75, 91, 136, 159
diarrhoea, 155
diets, 33, 98
dirtiness, 36
dissimulation, 38, 62, 67, 141
divorce, 27, 43, 46, 83, 88, 104, 137
dominant mother, 50, 61
dominant rôle, 50, 60, 67–8, 73, 135
dreams, 26, 27, 28, 29, 41, 42, 46, 47, 58, 59, 64, 65, 70, 71, 80, 81, 94–6, 131, 135, 154, 158, 168, 169, 172, 176, 177, 178, 179, 181, 182, 183, 184
drugs, 22, 23, 97, 98, 105

eating, 30–8, 177
eczema, 70, 101
Electra Complex, 77
emotional deprivation, 30, 32, 51, 75
emotional involvement, 65
emotional problems, 7, 14, 17, 18, 21, 24, 37, 41, 47, 97, 98, 99, 104, 105, 113, 134, 154, 176, 187
erections, 40, 41, 46, 56, 57, 65, 169, 173, 174
ethics, 114, 117
extrasensory experiences, 24

family, 46, 86, 87, 88, 132–3, 144, 154–87
fantasies, 64, 80, 165, 166, 171
father-figures, 43, 46, 51, 52, 81, 131
fathers, 20, 21, 31, 43, 44, 45, 46, 48, 50, 51, 53, 54, 58, 59, 60, 61, 62, 63, 75, 76, 77, 78, 80, 81, 83, 88, 89, 102, 103, 104, 107, 121, 122, 127, 131, 132, 142, 143, 144, 149, 152, 154–86
fear of flying, 71
fear of men, 176
feeding, 30–6
fees, 37, 115–16, 119, 124, 129, 132, 137, 138, 152
fixations, 65, 77
follow-ups, 71, 109–10, 145–53
forgetting, 143, 152, 177
frankness, 139–44
frequency of sessions, 73, 117, 123, 126
Freudian slips, 47, 74, 93, 185
frigidity, 27, 28, 29
frustration, 69, 71

gang-bang, 46
genitals, 41, 62
gimmick therapy, 110
girlie magazines, 58, 66
group therapy, 150, 155
grouping, 67–8
guilt, 24, 32, 48, 53, 55, 58, 60, 64, 71, 73, 77, 82, 83, 88, 94, 117, 122, 131, 139, 142, 165, 169, 172, 174, 176, 186

hatred, 73, 75–81, 123
hatred of brother or sister, 79, 81
hatred of children, 50, 176, 183
hatred of father, 29, 51, 80, 81, 103, 122, 123, 175, 177
hatred of men, 43, 62, 65, 70, 122

hatred of mother, 57, 81, 123
hatred of son, 76, 77
hatred of women, 43, 57
hay-fever, 21, 100, 101, 103
headache, 70, 97, 99, 104, 143
herpes, 101
homosexuality, 37, 43, 47, 49–56, 75, 87, 103, 135
hormones, 49, 50
hospital, 28, 38, 163, 179
hostility, 19, 51, 52, 56, 59, 61, 70, 71, 73, 74, 95, 103, 114, 118, 119, 123, 124, 125, 137, 148
hypnosis, 7, 18, 25, 31, 58, 59, 61, 82, 84, 85, 93, 102, 105, 107, 107–10, 111, 112, 114, 116, 120, 122, 125, 130, 137, 146, 148, 154–87
hypochondria, 111

identifying, 76, 89
impotence, 40, 53, 56–63, 134–5, 138
incest, 45
incest law, 45
incest taboo, 45–8
incestuous feelings, 44, 46, 48, 89, 131, 158, 165, 169, 171–4
independence, 130, 131, 132, 149
indoctrination, 105
ineffectual men, 50, 66
infatuation, 127–8
inferiority feelings, 37
infertility, 40, 90
inhibitions, 41, 44, 51, 175
insecurity, 63, 85, 100, 127, 152
insight, 140
insomnia, 63, 70, 98, 175
instant cures, 114, 118, 120, 126–8, 150
instincts, 9–11, 15, 19, 39, 40
interpretation, 96, 100
irritation, 101, 105, 135

jealousy, 48, 60, 75–81, 89, 136
Jews, 151
jobs, 76, 92, 93–4, 106, 149
jokes, 93

kissing, 44, 51, 93, 156, 159, 165

Laius Complex, 77, 188
lateness, 59, 61, 73, 115, 125, 160
lesbianism, 47, 51, 183
listening, 129
losing things, 175
love, 32, 43, 46, 47, 51, 54, 76, 89, 142
love inability, 32, 47, 48, 51, 52, 62, 75, 89
love-substitutes, 32

manipulation, 60, 63, 83, 117, 130
marriage, 45, 51, 65, 66, 79, 83, 86–8, 93, 94, 95, 106, 121, 134–7, 175
masochism, 73, 114, 118
masturbation, 45, 47, 57, 60, 160, 164, 165, 171, 173, 182
meanness, 37
menstruation, 44, 46
migraine, 70, 104
mothers, 20, 21, 23, 31, 35, 36, 37, 42, 43, 45, 46, 47, 48, 50, 54, 57, 58, 59, 60, 61, 63, 65, 73, 76, 77, 78, 80, 81, 82, 83, 85, 88, 102, 104, 107, 121, 129, 131, 132, 133, 135, 142, 143, 144, 148, 149, 152, 155–86
mouth, 30, 41, 161
murder, 29, 35, 68, 72, 76–81, 93, 95, 105, 122, 168, 169, 172, 182

nail-biting, 58, 70, 100, 101, 103
negativeness, 29, 91
negative transference, 51, 61, 70, 119, 123, 124, 125, 149, 150
nervousness, 24, 52, 63
neuroses, 34, 118, 124, 136, 139
neurotic choice, 88, 151–3

obsession, 31, 110, 138
obsessive cleanliness, 37
Oedipus Complex, 76–7
orgasmic inability, 40, 57, 62–4, 65, 70, 102, 130, 138
orgasms, 41, 55, 57, 63, 64, 66, 138
overweight, 33–4, 93, 104, 105, 130, 148

pain, 21, 28, 73, 96, 97, 143, 161, 163,

191

165, 168, 177, 186
painful sexual intercourse, 65–6
'painkiller' drugs, 22, 97, 99
pair-bonding, 86
panic, 127
paralysis, 105
paranoia, 55, 74–5, 114, 163
parental attitudes, 82–5, 154–87
parent-figures, 118
parents, 13, 15, 20, 21, 27, 30, 31, 32, 37, 38, 39, 40, 41, 43, 45, 46, 47, 48, 50, 57, 58, 59, 60, 69, 70, 73, 74, 75, 76, 77, 80, 81, 82–5, 87, 88, 91, 95, 103, 104, 110, 119, 121, 125, 129–34, 139–44, 154–87
passive father, 50, 73, 88
passivity, 50, 72, 73, 88, 135
patience, 69
pecking order, 68–9
penis, 36, 39, 40, 42, 43, 47, 49, 61, 65, 81, 162, 171, 172, 173, 174, 177, 179, 180, 181, 185, 186
penis-envy, 41, 42, 172, 174
perfect children, 84
persecution, 74
phallic symbols, 71
phantom pregnancy, 88
phobias, 26, 28, 107–10, 147, 151, 155, 176
policemen, 46, 178
politeness, 141
positive transference, 51, 123
possessiveness, 48, 58, 63, 84, 87, 130, 131
potential, 104, 153
pre-birth memories, 25
precipitating factors, 97, 101, 104, 106
pregnancy, 26, 28, 40, 44, 78
premature ejaculation, 57, 61
presenting symptoms, 61, 63, 145
previous lives, 24, 25
procreation, 88, 106
projection, 27, 56, 74, 76
promiscuity, 87
prostitutes, 65
psoriasis, 101
psychogenic problems, 98, 100
psychotropic drugs, 98

puberty, 41, 46, 49, 65, 127, 148
pubic hair, 49
pulling own hair out, 120
punishment, 24, 45, 60, 71, 73, 94, 132–3, 144, 151, 158, 177, 179

recollection, 30–1
referrals, 112–13
refusal to eat, 32
regression, 24, 25, 176, 187
rejection, 70, 120, 123, 125, 138, 150–3, 188
relationship problems, 51, 62, 103, 104, 110
relatives, 129–34
relaxation, 50, 186
religion, 48, 91, 140
repressed feelings, 19, 40, 44, 48, 57, 70, 71, 73, 75, 94, 100, 122, 123, 139
repressed wishes, 24, 37, 51, 75, 89, 94
resentment, 36, 60, 61, 70, 71, 75, 103, 124, 175, 177, 183
resistance, 93, 100, 112, 126, 141
responsibility, 152
results, 51, 52, 53, 54, 59, 60, 61, 63–4, 66, 92, 102, 103, 104, 109–10, 120, 126, 131, 136, 138, 139, 141, 142, 145–53, 175, 186–7
retarded ejaculation, 57, 61
revulsion, 60, 166
ridicule, 59, 60, 74
rôle reversal, 32
Roman Catholicism, 29, 44, 66, 140

sabotage, 59, 140
sadism, 68, 73, 118
security, 52, 87, 105, 116, 169, 170
seduction, 47
self-assertion, 137, 139–44, 155, 186
self-expression, 14, 139–44, 154, 186
self-destruction, 71, 182
self-punishment, 94
sex, 14, 15, 39–66, 131, 137, 149, 150, 164–75
sex education, 44
sex with animals, 64–5
sexual attitudes, 43, 44, 46, 50, 51,

192

62, 160, 179
sexual fallacies, 44
sexual fears, 44
sexual ignorance, 44, 160
sexual intercourse, 28, 40, 41, 44, 46, 47, 61, 63, 73, 102, 130, 131, 154, 169, 178, 187
sex magazines, 66
sexual problems, 34, 40, 41, 44, 61, 62, 65, 103, 128, 134
sexual repression, 44, 46, 96
sexual rôles, 49–50, 52, 59, 135, 178, 179, 185
sexual taboos, 46
shyness, 24, 60
siblings, 76, 78, 79, 80
silence, 127, 176
singles, 63, 83, 87, 88, 111
sisters, 45, 48, 60, 79, 131, 132, 164, 165
skin disorders, 100, 101, 102, 105
smoking, 30, 63, 101, 128, 147
social attitudes, 46
social work, 53, 72
sons, 45, 46, 51, 76, 77, 78, 80, 88, 89, 129, 130
speech impediment, 111, 130
spiritual healers, 130
spoiling, 79
stammer, 75
starting therapy, 73, 112–20, 124, 125–8
stealing, 59, 162, 170, 178
sterility, 40
stomach ulcer, 138
stomach upsets, 60, 143, 163, 186
stress, 105
stubbornness, 37, 58, 176
sublimation, 72
subservience, 141
sucking, 30
suggestion treatment, 105
suicide, 55, 72, 74, 176
survival, 10, 14, 15–7, 23, 39, 67, 69
symbolism, 43, 71, 96, 173
symptoms, 14, 21, 97–111, 130, 137, 143, 147

tension, 70

termination of therapy, 61, 73, 96, 117, 123, 124, 125, 131, 133, 137, 145–55, 186
territorial dominance, 14, 67, 188
territorial instinct, 9, 10, 67, 188
thalidomide, 23
therapeutic situation, 79–80, 121–5
thumb-sucking, 30
toilet training, 36, 37, 60, 181
toys, 49, 89
training, 31, 112, 113, 117, 154, 188
transference, 51, 61, 70, 79, 121–8, 131
tranquillisers, 63
traumas, 106, 161
trial period, 125–6

unconscious mind, 18, 23, 91–4, 95
unloving fathers, 51, 52, 62, 75, 89
unloving mothers, 57
unloving relationships, 50
urination, 10, 41

vagina, 42, 49, 60
vasectomy, 42–3
vegetarianism, 36, 130
vengeance, 32, 132, 143, 164
violence, 45, 60, 158, 162, 176–85
virginity, 48, 64, 65, 111
vomiting, 33, 66, 162, 177, 182
vomiting phobia, 28, 147

weak fathers, 50, 61, 66, 132, 135
wholistic therapy, 52, 101, 103
womb, 49
worry, 32, 33

young people, 129–34